AF413239

A LEAP OF FAITH

A LEAP OF FAITH

An Athlete's Journey to God

HUGH F. X. McMAHON

RESOURCE *Publications* · Eugene, Oregon

A LEAP OF FAITH
An Athlete's Journey to God

Copyright © 2023 Hugh F. X. McMahon. All rights reserved. Except for brief quotations in critical publications or reviews, no part of this book may be reproduced in any manner without prior written permission from the publisher. Write: Permissions, Wipf and Stock Publishers, 199 W. 8th Ave., Suite 3, Eugene, OR 97401.

Resource Publications
An Imprint of Wipf and Stock Publishers
199 W. 8th Ave., Suite 3
Eugene, OR 97401

www.wipfandstock.com

PAPERBACK ISBN: 979-8-3852-0272-0
HARDCOVER ISBN: 979-8-3852-0273-7
EBOOK ISBN: 979-8-3852-0274-4

10/16/23

Contents

CONTENTS

Acknowledgments

WITHOUT AN EDITOR, BOOKS are just random thoughts. Having a great editor is essential for clarity and flow. Joya Stevenson, Ph.D. kept me on track and her recommendations made the book seamless. I cannot thank her enough. A dear friend of fifty-five years, Dean Popps, urged me to write this book. He knew who I was and knows who I have become. He thought sharing my story would have a great impact on many. My loving wife, Bonnie, gave me the time and space to write. Bonnie and I traveled our own paths, and we believe those paths merged as God had designed.

Most importantly, I thank God. His unseen guidance through dark times, His constant love, and the depth of His mercy and forgiveness is unfathomable. Finally, I pray my sons, Mike, Brendan, James, and Matthew find the peace of God to bring them home safely to Heaven.

Preface

EVERYONE HAS A STORY. How did I come to be who I am? Many of the people I've known in my life are stoical and keep everything bottled up inside. Most men are unwilling to open up as it wouldn't be considered 'manly.' But, manly or not, it's really foolish to keep things inside that tear you up. Looking honestly at ourselves and seeing those choices we've made during our lives; we can clearly see the evil and good we've done. We can reject and repent of those evils and give thanks for the good we've done, all to God's glory. *My Journey* could be the catalyst for others to take that look within and decide for themselves if they are willing to share in their own journey. What I have written here is true.

The beginning of this book deals with my early life, while the parts that come later describe events that happened after my "awakening," if I can call it that. While at my most vulnerable point in life, I opened myself up to God and He answered me. God's love can't be fully explained but can be sensed and felt. Those who knew me in my early life wouldn't know the person I am today and those who know me now can't imagine that I was anything else than who I am today. God presented me with a choice; I chose Him and He hasn't disappointed. He placed me on the right path. The book also includes some short essays or thoughts that have come to me, usually in the middle of the night, either while praying or just lying in my bed wide awake.

I have shared some of these stories already in conversation. I felt compelled to write them down. I offer them, in this book, to assist others and to answer their questions about what is real and what is true.

In response to my reflections about God and the meaning of life, many react by remarking, "I never thought of that." One piece that has received an especially broad and favorable reception is "Reconciling with Your Past." Many fear to do so. They don't want to open old wounds, though they realize that must be done to be free from their past. This book is an act of reconciliation for you to heal the past and give hope and joy for the future.

Hugh McMahon

Fear and Freedom

Snow was falling gently onto my soft, cozy blanket, forming a fluffy pile. From the comfort of the carriage on our Brooklyn back porch, I was mesmerized by the sight of the white snow sprinkling down, almost like tiny fairies dancing in the air. At the tender age of two, the world seemed magical to me.

It was February of 1951, and I was very evidently in love with the falling snow. However, much to my disappointment, as I was engrossed in the scenery, the back door of the carriage suddenly swung open, and my mother emerged. Her eyes widened with concern, perhaps worried about me being outside in the cold for too long. She quickly unbuckled me from the carriage and gently carried me inside.

Although I was quite upset with this, I grew up learning that this was something my mother did out of love and worry only, and that was the beauty of having a loving and trustworthy mother.

This is my first recollection of my mother.

My father, however, was quite the opposite. His behavior was less predictable and trustworthy. He would suddenly become irritated or enraged. For example, while we were on holiday, he would show his true colors, sometimes in the worst way possible.

Birthday parties are times of joy and celebration. When it's for twins, it's doubly so. On July 4th, 1952, an incident occurred while we were in Coney Island to celebrate Independence Day, and my father's birthday. He and his brother were twins, born on the 4th. It was their fortieth birthday. My father had taken my older brother and I down to the beach early that day. He belonged to The Elmore Club, comprised mostly of blue-collar working men, who sought out an oasis during the sweltering summers to escape the hustle-bustle and heat of New York City.

My brother, John, was a year older than me, and my sister, Margaret, was a year younger. After us, more siblings came, all boys, and by 1958 there were five boys and my sister. Yes, we all were quite a handful.

We arrived around 10 o'clock, long before anyone else. I had assumed we were going to go down to the ocean to swim and play in the sand. The club was a large bungalow rather than a real beach clubhouse. It was weathered and crumbling, with multiple layers of peeling paint that seemed to paradoxically hold the structure together. It was situated about a block from the beach. My father had other ideas as to why we were there early. We had to clean up the unkempt clubhouse and police the surrounding area for trash. Not exactly the oasis I was hoping for, even at 3 ½ years of age. Grease-stained hot dog wrappers and cardboard beer coasters were littered in and around the club. Apparently, it was our job to pick them up.

As we were tidying up bits of trash off the concrete, my father was diligently hosing down the area to make it spick and span. Perhaps I was dawdling, or maybe I just missed the gum wrapper near my feet, but my father sprayed me with the hose. Getting sprayed by cooling water actually felt refreshing, and I mistakenly thought he was spraying me for fun and to cool me off. I was wrong. He began screaming at me to pick up the wrapper and to "hurry up about it." For the first time, it occurred to me that my father did not like me. This was in stark contrast to my mother's tender concern for me on the porch, as the delicate snowflakes had settled on me. That first run-in with my father and his temper stayed with me as much as that snowfall had. I began to feel wary of him that day.

There were worlds of difference between my parents. My mother was college educated, and my father had only finished the seventh grade. She was raised in a loving family unit. She was a woman of strong faith, as were her mother and siblings. They were very active in the Catholic Church in Brooklyn. My father's family went to church, but they were not overtly religious, as far as I recall. My mother's family seemed more focused on education and hard work, while my father's family was more focused on entertaining—and they were quite good at entertaining. My mother and father were polar opposites, just as my first wife and I were. They met after the war at a novena in their parish. One of my cousins told me a few years ago, that it had been an arranged marriage.

They never showed affection towards each other, at least, as far as my observations go.

(Coney Island July 4th, 1952. I'm second from the right on the bench, my brother John is to my left, and my sister Margaret, the 4th one in from the right in front of my mom. My father is in the back row over my right shoulder, and my mom is to his right.)

I developed a lifelong passion for sports in my childhood, and some of my fondest memories relate to games and athletic events. Three years after the incident in Coney Island with my dad, a neighbor living upstairs asked our mom if he could take my brother John and me to a Dodgers game. He was a police officer and a really nice guy. She said yes, and we went the next afternoon. My mom gave us each a dollar. That was a lot of money back then; in retrospect, she probably couldn't afford it. This was my second opportunity to go to a game at Ebbets Field. Ebbets Field, home to the Dodgers since 1913, was a raucous place. The Brooklyn Irish, Italians, Blacks, Polish, and Germans all gathered as one army to support their team, their "Bums," as the team was nicknamed. The beers, the cheers, the hisses and boos, the hot dogs, the laughter—all of this fun and tumult were to me, better than any circus.

The beautiful green grass and the blinding white of the Dodger uniforms completed the perfect scene. I loved the Dodgers and loved baseball.

(John (r) and me, 1954)

We got to our seats, and I was glued to mine for the entire game. I didn't even notice when John and our neighbor left for a few minutes. My brother came back with a hot dog and a Coke. The unbridled joy of the game, and all the surrounding festivities, were more captivating than food or drink. The Dodgers won, and we went home elated.

Even though I had lots of fun with friends and sports, my life at home was rough because of my dad's anger and suspicious nature. I longed for him to be my protector, someone I could confide in and seek solace from, but instead, a wall of mistrust loomed between us. I could never be my true self with him. Each time I tried to share my thoughts or feelings, it felt like stepping on a landmine, never knowing when his temper would explode, turning him against me.

That day, we all arrived home from the game late in the afternoon; laughter still echoing in our hearts, the joy making us forget how much time had passed. A number of the guys were playing stickball on the street outside of our home. My brother got to play. I wasn't picked. After a while, I got thirsty watching them. I then remembered; I had the dollar my mom had given me. I decided to go down the block to Joe's candy store and get a soda. Joe's sold everything: magazines, candy, pretzels, even sandwiches. I reached into the soda tub and swirled the ice-cold water around, looking for a Coke. After finding one, I paid Joe with the dollar, and he gave me 87 cents change, which I put in my pocket.

Billy, the block bully, confronted me as I left the store. He told me to give him some money for a soda. I said I didn't have any money. He said, "I saw Joe give you change, so hand it over." Billy was about five years older than me. With his James Dean look and attitude, he intimidated the younger kids. I was certainly afraid of him. I reached into my pocket and took out the change. He took it all and my soda. I walked home, mad as hell, but I couldn't do a thing about it. He had a reputation for beating people up, and I didn't want to be his next victim.

During dinner, my father asked how the game was. Excitedly, I said we won. He then asked if we had any change from the money our mom had given us. My brother reached into his pocket and gave him what he had left. I said I didn't have any change. John, not trying to be mean, said that I hadn't bought anything at the game. My father asked about the money, and I told him that Billy, the bully, had taken the money and my soda from me outside of Joe's. I thought he believed me.

After dinner, the older guys were playing stickball, including Billy. My father went out and confronted him. I was standing on the curb, watching as Billy repeatedly lied to my father. Billy was standing there, with a look of astonishment, with his palms up, shaking his head as if he was completely innocent. Finally, my father turned and told me to get into the house. He followed me in and gave me a beating for lying to him.

My father believed Billy and not me. He spanked me for a while and then told me to get to bed. I promised myself, then and there, I would never tell him the truth again if it meant avoiding a beating. I didn't trust him and I was in fear of him. I also never forgot Billy.

A few months passed and I, evidently, again did something to tick him off. I can't remember what it was, but I knew another beating was imminent. Well, I was wrong. Rather than a beating, he packed a bag, a brown A&P paper bag, tossed some of my clothes into it, and threw me out of the house. Here I was, a six-year-old, thrown out onto the streets of Brooklyn. Even though it felt eerie and disheartening, I remember feeling surprisingly okay with it.

(Six years old)

I walked to the corner and stopped, uncertain about which way to go toward Flatbush Avenue or toward Nostrand Avenue. I decided to go back and ask. When I arrived at the stoop, my mother was peeking through the venetian blinds. She waved at me to come in. I shook my head no. I was happy being out and away from him—my father. I asked her which way I should go. She raised the window a bit and told me to come in and go to the bedroom. She would bring me something to eat, and I should go to sleep. Reluctantly, I went back into the house. My fear heightened. I fell asleep wondering why my father didn't like me or want me. At the time, I was in parochial school, St. Jerome's, and learned about God as Father. I reasoned that if my father didn't like or want me, why would this God?

(The home on the right I was thrown out of when I was six years old)

My father's behavior made me incredibly insecure. If only he had apologized and told me that he cared about me, that I mattered, then I could have forgiven him, even as a child. But due to his own insecurities, he couldn't offer me any kind of reassurance. I later found the unconditional love I'd been seeking, from God the Father. And thankfully, my mother and my teachers were supportive and consistently kind. My father did have his nice moments, as I'll go on to describe.

At the beginning of each school year, you hoped you would get a good nun. In 1956, I entered the third grade at St. Jerome's Catholic school, and Sister Mary Cabrini was assigned as our nun.

I didn't know her but liked her immediately. She was one of those rare nuns who smiled. If she asked me to do anything, I did it eagerly and with a sense of joy. I wanted to do my best and for her to be proud of me. This was also the same year you could try out to be an altar boy. Yes, back then, you had to try out. My brother, John, was already an altar boy and helped me with Latin. I made it through and was invested with fifteen others. Receiving a cassock and surplice was better than any Christmas gift. Being on the altar brought me closer to God, and I knew that was where I was supposed to be. I felt more at home there than I did in my own house. My mom was delighted and proud. My dad seemed to be okay with it. Looking back, I can see he was unhappy with his life. I can only suspect his father behaved toward him as he did toward me.

There were, however, a few instances when he let his guard down. One Saturday a month, he would go to work and get paid overtime for it. On one of these Saturdays, he came home while we were playing in the street. A lot of the boys had small plastic cap rockets. You filled them with exploding caps and tossed them into the air. Upon landing, the caps would explode. Everyone wanted theirs to erupt with the biggest explosion. My dad asked about mine. I told him I didn't have one. He reached into his pocket and gave me a nickel. "Go get one," he said.

I couldn't believe it. Excitedly, I ran down to the candy store and bought one, along with a box of caps. I couldn't wait to toss mine up in front of everyone. I loaded it up with caps and made sure everyone was watching. I launched it into the air. It never came down. It got caught on a branch high up on a nearby tree. I couldn't climb up high enough to get it. One toss, and it was gone. My dad never asked about the lost cap rocket, and I didn't volunteer. That rocket stayed stuck in that tree for years. For all I know, it's still there. That was one of the rare moments that my dad seemed to care.

Looking back on those early years, I now realize that God had His hand on me. Despite the challenges at home, I found solace and purpose in serving as an altar boy and eventually joining the boys' choir. As with the altar boys, you had to try out for the choir. I didn't make it at first, but I always felt I could sing. A few months went by, and I went to the choirmaster, Mr. Renner, to ask if I could try out again. He told me to come the next morning before practice began. The choir practiced before school started. I got myself up early and left the house, not telling my parents where I was going. I arrived before any of the choir members. Mr. Renner told me to come up onto the stage. I sang a few chords and then a hymn. He smiled when I finished and then directed me to sit with the choir who had just arrived. I was floating on a cloud. My best memories were those days spent in church.

The nuns we had at St. Jerome's were Sisters of Mercy. Most of them were good people and really did try to help us. However, a few were not good people. Perhaps life had passed them by, or they were forced into the convent, or they took vows and regretted it. Whatever the reason, they seemed like they didn't want to be there and decided to take out their resentment on the children. I had a few nuns like this. They were authoritarian like my father and disciplinarians as well. No matter the subject they were teaching, they held the fear of God over my head. God, for me then, became an authoritarian figure, filled with punishment and retribution. The Catholic Catechism was the rule book and was also taught as an instrument of fear and intimidation. The 'fear' of the Lord meant you were supposed to be scared to death of Him and any who represented Him. The nuns and my father represented Him.

(John, Mom, and me)

Over the next few years, the beatings and the fears continued. My mother was helpless. She did all she could do to keep the peace, and kept us fed and clothed. When my father was at work, the atmosphere in the house was peaceful. Once he came home, a pall fell over everyone. We stayed out of sight and kept quiet. The basement was the only place to escape. Dinner was always a dreadful time as he would ask questions, and you prayed you wouldn't be asked any. I was getting adept at lying. So, I escaped a few times because of lies. But, there was no way to escape the beatings, especially when they got worse.

The Party, The Punishment

The most violent attack from my father happened when I was ten, after a birthday party and dinner with my grandmother. I was invited to a birthday party of a classmate. Since I had never been to a party outside of our house until that point, I was excited, though my excitement was tempered by caution. By this time, I could sense my father's moods. My mother had a gift for me, a shirt, that she had wrapped up. I don't know the reason, but my father was upset that I was going and told me to come right home after the party.

The party itself was a blast, filled with laughter, games, and the company of cherished friends. Although his command placed a damper on the party as I knew what awaited me when I got home.

(@ Grandma's for Easter 1959. L-R my father, Christopher, Patrick, John,
Stephen, and me)

Despite my father's stern instructions, I made a slight detour
on the way home from the party. My grandmother's home was two
blocks away, and she was on the porch rocking in a rocking chair
as I passed by. I went up onto the porch and sat for a while. She
was my mom's mom. She loved me and I felt it. I loved her as well.
I knew I had to get home, but this respite was welcome. I stayed
on the porch, rocking and talking to my grandmother for about
thirty minutes. My uncle, who was living with my grandmother at
the time, came out to ask if I would be staying for dinner. I knew
I shouldn't have, but my grandmother immediately answered for
me, "Yes." As my uncle phoned my parents to let them know I was
staying for dinner and that he would drive me home afterward, I
felt a mix of emotions. On one hand, staying with my uncle was
a breath of fresh air; his presence always brought comfort and

understanding. The dinner he prepared was delightful, filled with flavors and warmth that eased the tensions in my heart.

Yet, as the evening wore on, I couldn't shake the apprehension that gnawed at me. Thoughts of what awaited me at home weighed heavily on my mind, and the sense of conflict intensified. I knew that walking back into that household would unleash a torrent of anger and suspicion from my father, causing the joyful moments with my uncle to feel like a distant dream.

When I reached home, I was instantly greeted by my father's deadly glare. He didn't say anything, just instructed me to go directly to bed. It was about 8 PM. I didn't sleep one minute that night. I knew he was going to come in and drag me from the bed for another beating. The next morning was Sunday, I got up and went to 9 o'clock Mass. He always went to the 10:15 Mass. After he arrived home, we had breakfast. He began yelling at me for not coming home immediately after the party. I was sitting down at the end of the table. He, for some reason, was standing up and continuing to yell. I was going to get hit. And then it came. I turned my head, and he hit me in the head—with a knife. The pain was searing, and panic surged through me as I grabbed my head, feeling its wetness. Looking at my hand, I saw it covered in blood, and fear gripped my heart.

He yelled at me to get into the bathroom and I complied, my mind racing with confusion and terror. I got to the bathroom, and he bent me over the tub and began running water. We had a tub with one of those rubber hoses coming out of the faucet. He placed the hose over my head; all I could see was red blood pouring down the drain. He called for my older brother to get a taxi. After a few minutes, a taxi was outside, and my father and I were in it, headed for Caledonia Hospital in Brooklyn. I had a towel on my head, and he said to keep pressing down on it. He then said something I'll never forget. "If the doctor asks you what happened, tell him that you and your brother were wrestling, and he threw you into a radiator." I knew at that moment he was scared. I had never seen him scared before, and he covered his fear with lies.

When the doctor finally examined me, he asked how it happened. I told him my brother and I were wrestling. I don't think he believed me. He stepped to the side, blocking my father from view. He quietly asked again. I told him the same story but realized something at the same time. Though I lied to the doctor, I had some semblance of power over my father. The doctor shrugged, said "ok," and stitched my head up. Nine stitches, if memory serves me right. Rather than fearing my father any longer, I just hated him. I wasn't alone in receiving beatings, but I got the lion's share. I wanted out of that house and away from him. Up until that point, I assumed all homes and families were the same as ours. I figured every kid got a beating and got them often. Seeing some of the dads in the neighborhood laugh with their sons and now and then, hug them, made me realize I was wrong. And it also led to a sting of pain in my heart; the affection I didn't receive from my own father made me envious of the ones who did, and to be honest, a little sad too.

Stubbornness. It is the Titanic trait of the Irish. I could be stubborn, and maybe this was my way of holding some power, given how vulnerable I felt. Even when we know we are wrong, we'd rather go down with the ship than admit it. My mom was a good cook, not a chef, but a good cook. One evening, when I was around eleven years old, she made dinner and served lima beans as one of the vegetables. I hated lima beans. They tasted like waxed green cardboard. Now, I know others swear by them but not me. We had to take something of everything cooked. I was expected to put some of those beans on my plate. I attempted to pass the bowl without taking any, but my father wouldn't have it. I placed the beans on my plate carefully so that they wouldn't touch any of the other food on the plate.

I ate everything on the plate except those beans. When it was time to get up and bring the plates over to the sink, I wasn't allowed to get up until those beans were eaten. Dessert came, and everyone else had dessert. I sat, staring at those beans. With dessert over, everyone got up and went on to study or take a bath. I kept on, sitting with the uneaten, unappetizing beans. My mother and father were in the living room watching television. I knew I couldn't toss the beans out as my father would have inspected the garbage, and we didn't have a dog!

Ten o'clock came and everyone was getting ready for bed.

"You're not going to get up from that table until you eat those beans." My father shouted, angrily, as he went upstairs to go to bed. Eleven o'clock. Midnight. One o'clock. It was just me staring at those beans. I was not going to eat them. They were beginning to shrivel up. Perhaps by morning, they would have shriveled enough to disappear, I thought. At two o'clock, my father came downstairs for some cookies and milk. He came into the kitchen and got the milk out of the refrigerator. He looked at me and came to the table.

"Those beans are going in your body in the next thirty seconds. You might want to decide right now where they are going in." He was serious.

Swallowing my pride was nearly as difficult as swallowing those beans. I finally ate them.

"Now, you never have to eat lima beans again, but when I tell you to do something, I want it done," he demanded, slamming his hand on the table. "Now get up to bed."

I promised myself that if I had children, I wouldn't do this to them. I wouldn't bully or intimidate or force compliance. I never did. I've told my sons to at least try to eat what is put before them. If you don't like it, you never have to eat it again. I, however, have never served them lima beans!

The atmosphere in the house made having fun or friends there hard. His constant tension and fear lingered like a dark cloud, dampening joyous moments. However, as my twelfth birthday approached, my mother surprised me with a glimmer of hope. It was to be on a Friday night, and I could invite ten or so friends, all boys. By the eighth grade, all parties were co-ed. Mine was not to be. My father would have put the kibosh on having any girls over to the house. As it was, I invited about ten guys. No one showed up. I went to bed without cake, ice cream, or friends. I have never liked my birthday ever since.

My mother, I believe, was sympathetic to my plight, our plight. I remember sitting on the floor one day with my back against the sofa. My mom was on the sofa reading a book. She knew how I felt about my father and how I feared him. Suddenly, she reached over to me and stroked my head.

"If my father was still alive, your father wouldn't be like he is. My father wouldn't allow it."

Though it didn't lessen my fear of my father, it did comfort me to know my mom understood.

As mentioned earlier, I used to think of God as an authoritarian, perhaps based on my dad's example. Why would He be any different? After all, didn't God punish you for the things you did? Well, that was my mindset early in life. He'd never love me since everything I did, seemed to be wrong. As you will see in this book, my understanding of God evolved beyond this limited idea. God's relationship with me and everyone is quite different from what my dad modeled and how he related to me. It took time to learn about God and trust Him, but it was all worth it. In the meantime, I had to survive.

Then, basketball came along: my gateway to freedom.

Basketball, My Ticket Out

As mentioned earlier, I went to St. Jerome's parochial grammar school. St. Jerome's was a large school with nuns, Sisters of Mercy, teaching all grades. During my first few years, I was a reasonably good student. I liked learning and knowledge. For the most part, the nuns were good and kind. As aforementioned, I was an altar boy, a role which I loved and enjoyed immensely. There was always something very special about it, and I remained an altar boy until my junior year in high school. I resigned because of an insulting remark from my father. He told me that I looked like an idiot up on the altar since I was two feet taller than the priest and four feet taller than the other altar boys. Despite this comment, I loved being in Church. As I progressed through school, my grades got worse, and I felt as though I couldn't learn. Everyone was becoming smarter than I was, so I faked it and tried to stay out of the way. Once, when a book report was due, I hadn't read a book. I made up a book and an author in order to have something to turn in. I wrote about a fictitious book and got a B for it! Faking it was the new way of life for me.

Over time, I understood that my home wouldn't change, neither my father. So, getting out of the house was my goal—and staying out! Basketball was my way out. As there was only one school team, I was relegated to a team with older guys. Though I didn't play much, it was enough just to get an escape from the house. My older brother also played on the team, and he was one of the stars. I began to love the game and wanted to be included as a good player.

One year difference in age is a great deal when you're young. You're always the last guy picked and, even then, chosen with regret.

I began to grow and began to get better and improve at basketball. My father had no interest in my playing though he did have an interest in my older brother's playing. By my sophomore year in high school, I began to love the game. I was nearly 6'5," and I was getting picked to play more often. Most of the guys I played with in school were black guys, and they were nicer than some of the white guys I had grown up with at St. Jerome's. All they cared about was whether you could play ball. There was an unspoken rule back then, that you didn't play with blacks. I thought it was stupid then, and always thought it was stupid. I started to have fun; for the first time in my life. I liked the challenge, but more importantly, I liked being accepted. Basketball became my life, my breath, my blood.

Erasmus Hall was a huge public high school in Brooklyn, known for their great basketball teams. Both my brother and I went for tryouts. He was a senior and I was a junior. He was a better player, but we played different positions. I knew he'd make the team and I prayed I would. Each evening at dinner, my father would ask us how tryouts were going. We both said, "okay," without elaborating. As it turned out, I made the team, and my brother didn't. Instead of being happy for me, my dad was upset that John hadn't made the team. He told me to, "go and ask that coach why Johnnie didn't make the team and you did!" I didn't ask.

The day I made the team is seared into my memory, with a mix of nervousness and excitement. As I arrived at the tryouts, I saw that only a few spots were open on the team. Most of the team members were holdovers from the previous year's squad. Hundreds of guys showed up to try out. After three weeks, the coach had narrowed down the prospects to ten. Three spots were left to complete the team. The members of the previous year's varsity team were on the sidelines, watching. Many of them had friends trying out and were cheering for them. I was alone. I knew no one. The coach, Bernie Kirshner, divided us evenly. I wanted this more than anything. Although I was scared, my love for playing and my absolute desire to make the team must have made an impression on the coach. We played for about forty-five minutes, and he told us to sit. He met with his assistant coach, Al Badain, for about five minutes.

"Thanks to all of you for coming out for the team. You made it to the last day. However, I can only select three of you for this year's team."

Had I done enough? Did the coach even notice me? These thoughts were racing through my mind. *Please call my name*, I prayed.

"If I call your name, go over and pick up a uniform," the coach continued. There were three uniforms on the bench across the court. "Hugh McMahon, go get a uniform."

I can't tell you how I felt. To this day, I am moved, shaken, and proud. To hear your name called when you have wanted something so badly is overwhelming. I think now of the Bible verse that says, "Israel, the LORD who created you, says: 'Do not be afraid—I will save you. I have called you by name—you are mine.'" Surely God had His hand on me then, though unbeknownst to me at that time.

I walked over and picked up a uniform with the number thirty-four on it. There were two sets of uniforms: one for home games and one for away games. There was also a warm-up jacket to complete the set.

As the coach called out two more names after mine, the world around me seemed to fade into the background. The cheers of the other players, the sound of basketballs bouncing became a distant murmur. My heart pounded in my chest, and a rush of euphoria washed over me. It felt as if I was walking on a cloud, a feeling of pure elation that I had never experienced before.

In that moment, nothing else mattered. The struggles at home, the weight of responsibilities, and the pain I had carried seemed to momentarily dissipate. All that existed was the overwhelming joy of making the team. The realization that I had earned my spot among a group of talented athletes filled me with an indescribable sense of pride and accomplishment.

I couldn't help but repeat to myself, "I made the team! I made the team!" It was a mantra that encapsulated the magnitude of the moment and the hope it brought for a brighter future. Basketball had become my escape, my refuge, and now, being part of the team represented the opportunity for a new beginning.

The walk home was amazing. As I passed several apartment buildings, some younger kids played outside. They were about thirteen years old. They knew I was trying out as they asked me every day without fail, how it was going. When they saw me walking with the uniforms, they were nearly as excited as I was. "Way to go! You made the team." I can't imagine that winning an Academy Award could be better than this. These kids were cheering me on and were truly happy for me. Here's the kicker. They were all black kids. In 1964, there was an undertone of racism in New York, but that barrier was dramatically diminished if you were a ballplayer. New York was changing. White flight began in earnest as many blacks were leaving the South and heading to northern cities. Perhaps some of these kids came from the South, yet they didn't care that I was a white guy. Walking through their neighborhood, I was something special because I made the team. They knew how good Erasmus's basketball was and hoped that someday, they would be walking home with a uniform. Arriving on my block, it was *ho-hum*. Perhaps the white guys on the block had other priorities or perhaps jealousies, but they didn't express a single compliment or cheer me on.

There was no one at home when I arrived. My mom was teaching, my father was at work, and the others were in school. I walked upstairs holding my uniforms in my hands as if holding a newborn. I placed the uniform and warm-up jacket on the bed and just looked at them. I still couldn't believe it. I made the team.

I was expecting someone to say something, but no one did, and I didn't volunteer anything. As I left for school the next day, I told my mom that I had basketball practice after school. She smiled.

"You made the team?"

"Yeah."

"Don't be late for dinner." That was it.

Things never got any better in the house, but at least I was out as often as possible. Foolishly, I was more interested in playing than studying. I had no idea that you had to maintain good grades to stay on the team. I found out the hard way. Once the grades came out, I was off the team. My head was spinning. How could I live without basketball? Two days after the grades came out, I was playing in a pickup game and broke my ankle. I had time to reflect. I vowed never to be in this position again. I spent the next six weeks on crutches. It was hard getting around the campus but even harder watching the team play and win every game that year. They won the City Championship, going undefeated. I missed out on a great experience and told myself it wouldn't happen again. I didn't know what my status would be for next season's team. Would I have to try it out again? If so, would I make the team? During the summer of 1965, I worked tirelessly to become a better basketball player. I didn't want to leave anything to chance.

By my senior year, I had improved, I was much better, and I had also grown to just over 6'5." I was still pretty skinny, but I wouldn't back down from anyone. Having had enough beatings growing up, I wasn't threatened by anyone trying to intimidate me. Our high school team was dominated by good black players; they were good guys as well. They accepted me as a teammate.

About three weeks before the start of my senior year, someone showed me an article in the New York Daily News. The article was about high school basketball in New York, and they interviewed coach Kirshner. He was asked about the upcoming year. He mentioned the names of his proposed starting team for the upcoming season.

"Coak Cannon was to be the center on the team, Ollie Shannon and Sol McMillon were to be the two starting guards, and Frank Payton and Hugh McMahon are to be the starting forwards."

I had absolutely no idea the coach thought of me in this way. The article further stated that I was 6'5" and weighed 180 pounds. I needed to put on 15 pounds if I didn't want to make a liar out of the coach. That was my thought. I started eating everything in sight. By the time school started, I was 175 pounds, and the coach asked if I had lost some weight!

I was fortunate to be a starter. That gave me a lot of confidence, and I hoped to continue playing in college. Though my grades were horrible, I held out hope. My father attended one game and never mentioned anything about it or my playing. I never asked him about it either.

We had a great year, and I learned a lot about basketball. Sadly, we lost the City Championship to DeWitt Clinton high school from the Bronx. They had one truly outstanding player, Nate Archibald, who went on to be an All-Star in the National Basketball Association (NBA).

A few years earlier, when I didn't make it into a Catholic high school, I was dejected as most of my classmates were accepted to one or another of the many Catholic high schools in Brooklyn. I was going to a public high school, and those in Catholic schools looked down upon public high schools. Public high schools were, for Catholics, a step down, and those Catholics not making it in were considered intellectually inferior. In hindsight, public high school was the very best thing that could have happened to me. It was eye opening.

The world was filled with people who weren't Irish Catholics or Italian Catholics. There were blacks, Jews, Protestants, Asians, and many more. Within two weeks of arriving at Erasmus Hall, I was friends with James Maci, a guy from the neighborhood, Rudolph VanExel, and Clayton Davis. James was Italian, and Rudolph and Clayton were black. We had a few classes together but always ate lunch together. Most of the lunch was spent listening to Rudolph's hilarious stories. Though they were black, and I was white, we all liked each other for who we were. We were not a clique, nor were there many of them at Erasmus. Unlike many of the Catholics, few of these guys were judgmental. Yes, it was a great experience and fortuitous that I went to public high school. As it turned out, more public high school graduates went to college than Catholic students, and more went to Ivy League schools as well. So much for perception. Looking back, I see that God had His hand on me in this way, too. It had pushed me to do the best I could with what made life easier, more bearable, for me. It had pushed me towards basketball, too. It had pushed me forward, reminding me that love, in all its forms, could be the ultimate remedy to the pain and emptiness I felt.

(# 34)

While the journey to find that love and acceptance was far from straightforward, I now understand that it wasn't about finding just any person. It was about finding someone who could see beyond the scars, someone who could love me for who I truly was, flaws and all. I wanted to be loved. I wasn't totally loved at home or in my house, but someday I would find that one person who would love me and that I could love. Where, who, when, and how, I had no idea, but I always believed there would be someone out there for me.

A Lifeline:
Colleges Were Interested Again

I HAD A FEW offers to play in college, but my grades prevented me from accepting any of them. I was lost. Is this it? I often wondered at the time. Then, out of nowhere, an option appeared. I could go to a prep school and improve my grades, hoping to get another chance to play in college—somewhere, anywhere. I attended a military prep school in Portsmouth, Virginia, for one year. Unbeknownst to me for years, my uncle, for whom I was named, paid the tuition for the school. Though I didn't particularly like the school, Frederick Military Academy, my grades improved dramatically; that was enough for me to receive several offers from colleges, some of them quite well known.

(Grandma, John, and I)

I liked being away from New York and hoped for an offer from a school that was not in the area. I received an offer to come and visit St. John's University in New York. Back then, it was a very prestigious basketball school and a very respectable university. The coach, Lou Carnesecca, was well known, and they always had good teams. I flew up from Virginia to New York for a visit. I stayed in the house for the weekend, hoping not to "get into it" with my father. He came to the meeting with me.

St. John's was nice, and the coach was very personable. He seemed very interested in my going there. He spoke to my father about the university's academics, social life, and sports facilities. Then, the coach turned to me and said the one thing he could have said to me to convince me not to go to St. John's. He said, "Hughie, as you know, we don't have dorms here at St. John's, so you can live at home!" He said this with such confidence as though it was a great selling point. My father was excited about it as I would once again be under his thumb. When I left, I had already resolved that I wasn't going to attend St. John's if it meant living at home. I held out hope that there would be an offer from another school away from New York.

As it happened, a meeting had been arranged the following day with the coach of Marquette University, Al McGuire, at La-Guardia airport in Queens. I remembered him from a talk he gave at our high school basketball awards dinner when I was a junior. He had a great sense of humor and was very direct. The star of our team, George Thompson, had accepted a scholarship to attend Marquette. My parents and I arrived at the airport about an hour before the flight was to depart. I was dressed in my Class A military uniform and waited nervously for Coach McGuire. He was coming to New York to see family and possibly recruit a ballplayer. The coach came and introduced himself. I could sense my father didn't like the coach, and my mother was cautious. I, on the other hand, liked him immediately. We talked for about twenty minutes, and he told me he'd be in touch. Then he left for the city. I thought about the meeting with Coach McGuire the entire flight back. I prayed. I wanted to go to college to play ball and wanted Marquette to be that place.

Arriving back at the barracks to no fanfare, I kept a low profile, determined to get the best grades I could and graduate. The next evening, after dinner, I went to a breakroom, where a basketball game was on the television. It was the National Invitational Tournament (NIT), played at Madison Square Garden in New York. One of the teams was Marquette. I had no idea they were playing prior to walking into that room. I watched the game; they won. They continued to win and advance in the tournament. I was excited that I knew their coach and their star, George Thompson. Sadly, they lost in the Championship game to Southern Illinois, whose star was Walt Frazier. I silently promised myself that if I could ever help Marquette win the NIT in the future, I would do it.

The barracks in which I lived had one phone booth in the courtyard. There were thirty-two cadets in each barrack. There were four barracks on our side of the campus. They were the athletic barracks. Cadets were allowed to make phone calls only at certain hours and briefly at that. This was also the phone booth that coaches would call to speak to athletic prospects. Two weeks after arriving back at school, the phone rang. I heard someone yell, "McMahon, phone call!" I ran out of the barracks, sprinting to the phone booth. It was the coach at Marquette offering me a full scholarship to attend Marquette. I couldn't believe it.

"Talk to your parents about it and get back to me."

"I don't need to. I know where I want to go. I want to come to Marquette."

"Are you sure?"

"Yes, I want to come and play for you."

"Ok, I'll send the paperwork in the morning. Sign it and send it back to me."

And with that, I was going to Marquette.

I called home right after I hung up with McGuire. My mother was concerned that I was calling so soon after I'd been at home. My father was concerned that I was calling because I suppose it was ruining his peace. I told my mother that I decided where I was going to go to school next year.

She coolly said, "Oh? And where is that?"

"Marquette."

"Well, OK."

"Do you want to tell dad?"

"No, you'd better do that."

She handed him the phone.

"What do you want?"

I told him I decided where I was going to go to school next year. He knew, with every fiber of his being, I was going to say St. John's. "I'm going to go to Marquette." I could feel the anger sizzling through the wires.

"What about St. John's?"

"I've decided on Marquette." He was getting madder.

"Marquette? Where the hell is Marquette?"

"Milwaukee."

"Milwaukee? Milwaukee! What?" My father was yelling into the phone.

"Wisconsin, Milwaukee, Wisconsin."

"Wisconsin? Wisconsin?! What the hell are you going to do if you get sick?"

"Huh, what do you mean?"

"There are no doctors on the other side of the Hudson! You call that coach back and tell him you changed your mind!"

"No, I'm going to Marquette."

He yelled into the phone, "You call that coach back and tell him you made a mistake!"

"No, I'm going to Marquette."

He slammed the phone down.

With that, I was free! I had just turned 18. Freedom. It was a great feeling. I was going to go to college, leaving that house for good and getting away to start a new life. There was a different kind of fear hitting me though. How would I act with all of this freedom? What will people expect of me? I decided to keep the walls up and continue to protect myself. I was heading into an environment of really smart people, and I couldn't let them know I was scared. Hell, I was going on 19, and I'd never had a date; never even talked to a girl. I was terrified. My whole life, I was just put into a box, never having the chance to fully explore what was outside the restricted premises. Needless to say, I did try my best, but emotionally, my walls were definitely built strong.

Before leaving for college, I spent the summer at home, and it quickly became evident that the tensions with my father hadn't abated. History repeated itself, and he tossed me out of the house once more. But this time, I didn't resist; in fact, I was relieved to leave. I held onto the belief that there was someone out there for me, someone who could understand and love me despite the walls I had built.

Ten years after this event, my mother told me the rest of the story. My father had gone to work the next day, still seething about my decision. He worked for the New York Post as a mailer. A mailer was a guy who took freshly printed papers and tied them up for delivery. Though he dressed nattily every day for work, once he arrived, he took off his suit and put on work clothes. My uncle, Lawrence, worked alongside him. During lunchtime, my father decided to find out more about Marquette University. He dragged Lawrence up to the sports writers' department and asked if there was anyone who wrote about college basketball. He was pointed in the direction of the writer. The writer looked up from his typewriter.

"Yeah, what is it?"

"Do you write about college basketball?" My father asked.

"Yeah, so?"

"Have you heard about this Marquette University?"

"Yeah. It's a good school with an up-and-coming basketball program. Why?"

"My kid is going there next year."

"Really? Good school."

"Yeah, he got a basketball scholarship."

The writer was now a bit more interested. He looked up, "Really? Who's your kid?"

"Hughie McMahon."

"Really? Hughie McMahon from Erasmus? He's your kid? He's going to Marquette? Good for him. I'll put it in the paper. What's your name?"

Well, according to my uncle, my father's disposition changed instantly and dramatically. He went back to work proudly telling everyone, "My kid is going to Marquette!"

It was a moment of validation and recognition that I had never experienced before. It was a rare and precious moment, a glimpse of a father's genuine approval and admiration. It felt like an affirmation of their worth, a reminder that I could achieve something remarkable.

Yet, beneath the elation, there was also a tinge of sadness. It was a bittersweet realization my father's approval seemed to come only when others recognized it.

Leaving New York

MILWAUKEE WAS A BIT intimidating. Not the city, but the academic environment. I soon realized that everyone was infinitely smarter than me. They spoke differently, acted differently, and seemed to be filled with confidence in their abilities. They had goals set before them. I had none of this confidence. Perhaps I had made a mistake. I did have my very first date and first kiss! By the third day at Marquette, I had made a good friend. He, Terry McQuade, and I became lifelong best friends. We were both scholarship basketball players from New York, both Irish and both Catholic. We hit it off right away. Terry was shy, had a great sense of humor and always looked for good in people. He was also a hell of a basketball player. The evening of that third day, there was a "smoker" at the student union. A smoker was just a get-together of incoming freshmen.

Terry and two other freshmen ballplayers were talking about their girlfriends and how they missed them. Having never had a date then, I decided to keep my mouth shut. Suddenly this guy comes out of nowhere and says to Dean Meminger, one of the two other players who was an All-American player in high school in New York, "Hey, you must be Dean Meminger!" He also looked at us and assumed we were ballplayers and introduced himself. He went on to talk about how great it was to have us there and if there was anything he could do or anyone we'd like to meet, he'd do his best.

FRESHMAN BASKETBALL TEAM
Back Row: T. Flynn (Asst. Coach), T. McQuade, B. Bromstead, H. Ray
monds (Coach). **Front Row:** H. McMahon, D. Meminger, R. Black, T.
Sonnenberg.

I thought this would be a good opportunity to meet a girl. So, pointing, I asked if I could meet a blond girl that was standing across from us. As I pointed, he flew away to corral her, without a hint of hesitation. My knees were knocking, and my mouth dried up. I was panic stricken. He came over with two girls: the blond and a brunette. The blond was very pretty, but the brunette was drop-dead gorgeous and took away my breath instantly. He introduced me to the blond, and Terry got the brunette! It did feel like a sting, but I focused my energy towards the blond with me. We chatted for a while about nothing that struck me as important enough to remember. But, taking my chances I suggested we go for a beer.

"We're not twenty-one."

"No problem. I know a place."

We left the student union and went across the street to the Knights of Columbus Hall (K of C). I found out you could get a beer there as they usually didn't "card" you. We entered the hall and went downstairs to the bowling alleys. There was a bar there with a few tables. Terry grabbed a table as I went up to the bar.

"Four beers."

"You got ID?"

I pulled out my wallet and showed him a draft card; a real draft card from a friend of mine back in Brooklyn. He was going into the Army and didn't need it any longer. He was twenty-one. I paid for the beer and brought them to the table. I felt like a big shot. The girls were pleasantly surprised, as was Terry. We had two rounds of beers and left. The girls had to be back in the dorm by ten-thirty. Their dorm was three blocks from the K of C. As we began to walk, the blonde slipped her arm into mine, and we walked up Wisconsin Avenue toward the dorm. Panic set in again. I questioned myself as to whether I should kiss her. With each step, I went from no to yes. What would she think? Would she think I was too bold? If I didn't kiss her, or at least try, would she think I was a nut? My mind was racing.

As we approached 18th Street where her dorm was, I was hoping for a reprieve. She provided it by suggesting we walk another block or two. Phew! When we had walked those two blocks, I had made the decision to kiss her. I didn't want to be too bold, so I decided to kiss her on the forehead. That would be gentlemanly. Well, we stopped next to a parked car, and I leaned against it. She came close and I bent down to kiss her again on the forehead. She put her left hand around my neck and pulled me down to her and the next thing I knew, she has her tongue in my mouth! I didn't know what to think. "What kind of girl is this? Is she a hooker?" We kissed for what seemed like a minute. I couldn't catch my breath. Once she released the kiss, like a plumber's plunger unclogging a sink, I gasped for a big breath. I believe she thought that it was an invitation to her to come back for more! I laugh at it now but, for me, back then it was truly an experience. I was scared to death but things went smoothly. In fact, talking to a girl wasn't as daunting as I thought it would be.

One thing I did notice was that though Marquette was a Catholic school, many of the students didn't attend Mass. I never ever thought about missing Mass. How could these kids, being so intelligent, think they need not go to Mass?

My one saving grace was that I still had basketball. Once on the court, I felt at home. All the players on the varsity and the three other scholarship freshmen players were better than I was. I knew it, but they didn't. I had to "act" once again. Early on, I got a reputation for being a tough guy. I wasn't tough at all, but if that's what they wanted, that's what I provided. Wanting to be accepted can be a fatal drug. I played on that "tough guy" image, and it seemed to work. Getting my front two teeth knocked out early in the season and not complaining about it added to the tough guy mystique. Perhaps all the beatings I received as a kid prepared me for the rough and tumble of college basketball. In any case, this is the attitude I projected.

That tough guy attitude and abrasive behavior, however, were not playing well with the coaches, especially the varsity coach. I was cutting classes. This wasn't high school or military school, and nobody was keeping tabs on me, at least not on a daily basis. I was lost in the fog of academia. I thought basketball would be enough to get me through. I was an academic and social mess. One morning I was called to come to the office of the varsity coach. Not knowing what he wanted, I was excited that he'd want to see me. I walked into his office self-assured. When I left, I was scared to death.

"What's your father's number at work?" McGuire asked, in an almost demanding tone.

"Whitehall 4–9000, extension 273." Holy crap, I thought, he's calling my father.

"John McMahon? This is coach McGuire at Marquette. You need to talk to your kid. He's breaking my balls!"

I couldn't believe anyone would talk to my father this way. I was paralyzed as McGuire handed me the phone. McGuire didn't need to ask what my father said as he could hear every word. My father was screaming. "What the hell is wrong with you? I don't want that coach calling me again." There was more to it, but that was the gist of the conversation. I sheepishly handed McGuire the phone back.

"Now get the hell out of here and act like you're supposed to. You're in college!"

I left wondering if I should just go down and sign up for the military. I sure as hell wasn't going home. I began questioning everything and coming up with few answers. Knocking a chip off of your own shoulder is hard; knocking off a boulder is nearly impossible, yet I knew I had to do it. I began whittling away at it. It took a long time for it to be completely gone. By "boulder," I mean my self-protective shell with the posture of invulnerability: my tough guy attitude. It was sabotaging me.

The tough guy attitude didn't help in the classroom. I was lost. Everything was going over my head. High school Biology wasn't college Biology, not by a long shot. Philosophy and Theology weren't any better. I tried reading the textbooks, all to no avail. Fortunately, one of the senior players on the team, Mike Curran, took me aside and gave me some very good and sound advice. He helped me navigate the academic highways. He told me to take a deep breath and relax. He said I should take courses that interested me and avoid the ones that didn't. I settled on Philosophy. I'm thankful to him to this day.

Though I had had my first and only date, I was still clueless as to the opposite sex. My first kiss was definitely a confidence booster, but I remained shy, which many, I found out later, believed to be aloofness. There were many beautiful women, nice women, kind women, and even funny women. Not ever having been exposed to any women, I was more than intrigued but still shy. Maybe, just maybe, that "one" I had hoped for and believed to be out there for me was here. As it was, I sunk back into basketball as it was my comfort zone.

When my grades came, they weren't pretty. I was determined to do better in the second semester. I did, but I still needed to complete one course over the summer to retain my scholarship. My mother came to the rescue. She was a teacher and helped me through the course. Of all things, it was a Theology course. I'll talk about that more later.

Upon returning for my sophomore year, I had a better understanding of college life, and the basketball program. But I still had no clue about dating or even approaching a woman to talk about anything but basketball. I loved basketball more than ever, loved the team, and loved the school and all its benefits. I was recognized though I was far down the bench as a player. I played with a reckless abandon all the time, whether it was in practice or in the game. People seemed to like my fearlessness, but I wasn't getting much playing time. I wanted to have an impact, but it wasn't in the cards. It still felt like I was watching the game, and had no big part in it, at least not one that was widely recognizable. At the end of the season, there was an awards banquet where players were given their Marquette Varsity "M" letters for playing. Believing that everyone on the team would get one, I fully expected to get my letter so long as they played a significant amount of time during the season. I was crushed when I didn't. There wasn't a numerical standard that needed to be met to qualify for a letter, but I believed getting into the games and playing was enough. It wasn't. Character meant a lot and I was lacking in it. As I left the banquet, I did a great deal of soul searching. I vowed to change, and I did. I would no longer carry that chip on my shoulder, that chip of being only a tough guy. I was going to be a ballplayer first.

I did, however, still have outbursts aimed at no one in particular. It was a tough period for me, as nothing made sense to me. The anger bursts, I suppose, were also a reflection of the void in my heart. But the thing about these outbursts is that no one really understands them, and they also have every right to not tolerate them too. So, when they became visible, people started pointing them out, and McGuire was the first to do so. McGuire had had enough of these and sent me to see one of the professors in Psychology. Maybe that was his way of helping me. That day, Al McGuire called me to his office and handed me a card saying, "I want you to go see this guy. Call him."

I went and met with the professor. I didn't have much to lose anyways. He had a doctorate in psychology and was head of the department. I had no idea why I was there to see him. We talked for about two hours, and I left. I didn't think anything of it nor did I think anything would come of it. At a basketball practice the next week, I had another blowup.

McGuire yelled something at me that stopped me in my tracks. "Hughie, I'm not your father!"

I was speechless as I immediately knew what he was talking about. The professor analyzed me and concluded that I hated my father and authority. He was right. No doubt he shared this with McGuire, and I'm glad he did. It was the only meeting I had with the professor. Looking back, I wish I had had more meetings, but none were scheduled, and I didn't think about asking for more.

Toward the end of my sophomore year, I met a girl to whom I was instantly drawn. She had so much of what I had dreamed about. Was it her? Was she the "one"? Though she was a senior, I mustered the courage to ask her out. When she said, "I'd love to," I was walking on a cloud. This was her! She was from Nebraska, tall with jet black hair and ice blue eyes. I was convinced after going out for two months. I could think of nothing but her, not even basketball. As it happened, she broke my heart and got engaged to a former boyfriend at school. I was crushed, to say the least. In retrospect, it was puppy love, but being in a real relationship had a significant impact on me. I began dating from that point onwards, but for all the wrong reasons with all the wrong women. I was on a glorious slide to Hell and did not know it; or at least I didn't admit it. I was caught up in the sexual revolution of the 1960's. "Friends with benefits" was the game, and I was participating—with gusto. Basketball was taking a back seat to bedrooms and saloons. The parties and conquests were an aphrodisiac I had not experienced before nor expected.

I did, however, change my attitude toward playing. My playing time increased. I had promised myself to do whatever it was the coach wanted me to do and not complain about anything. My grades went up as well. I was riding high in my third year, and everything was falling into place. I was recognized, popular; one of the guys. In mid-season, an article appeared in the local newspaper, The Milwaukee Journal, featuring me. The author extolled my virtue of being an enforcer. It only took a day to have that moniker stick. I was now the "Enforcer." An enforcer is one who doesn't back down from confrontations. I had to live up to it, as this is what fans expected of me; to play with ferocity and reckless abandon. To be honest, at the time, I relished it all, the image and reputation. It was a wonderful year in my life, and I thought it would never end. We had a great season and received an invitation to the NCAA tournament but turned it down. Coach McGuire felt our placing in Ft. Worth, Texas, was an insult. As a result, he chose to accept the invitation to go back to the National Invitational Tournament (NIT) in New York's Madison Square Garden. I remember what I had said to myself back in military school while watching Marquette lose in the final game to Southern Illinois. "I hope I can help Marquette win the NIT someday." Well, we won it in 1970!

(I am # 42 NIT@ Madison Square Garden vs. LSU)

Finding My Way: Young Adulthood

I MET A WONDERFUL young woman toward the end of that season and we began a long relationship. We had met the year before in French class but she was in a relationship. She was from North Carolina, a blond with a beautiful smile and a great sense of humor. She was also very intelligent. I was engaging is real conversations and not just spouting lines. We had wonderful times together and even got engaged. Though I cared deeply for her and loved her in some way, I knew she was not the "one." Further, there were chinks in my armor of which I was aware. Being faithful in a relationship is paramount. I failed at this. Though I knew we had to break up, it hurt. It hurt a lot.

An Old Grudge in Brooklyn

THROUGH A TWIST OF fate, I learned about the essence of forgiveness over the summer. It seemed like God set me up so that I could take the moral high road. During the summer months, I worked as a Pinkerton security guard at the thoroughbred horse tracks in New York. Terry McQuade, my best friend, and teammate got us jobs there through Gene McIntyre, the father of Kenny and Bobby McIntyre, two great basketball players at St. John's. Gene was an executive at Pinkerton's and had known Terry's family. Together, we would work the race circuit: Aqueduct, Belmont, and Saratoga tracks, and we made decent money doing it. In the evenings, there was always time for basketball games.

Foster Park in Brooklyn was a famous basketball park, and only a few blocks from our house. During the week, nearly every evening there were games going on at the six courts. Court number one was the premier court. If you got picked to play, you knew you made it. By the time I was a junior at Marquette, I had made it.

One evening, we were playing with a crowd of about 150 spectators. Several really good Black players came from various parts of Brooklyn to play against the locals. I was chosen, and we played for what seemed like hours. I really don't remember who won, but I do remember something from that evening.

After we finished, I noticed that a softball game was finishing on the other side of the fence from the basketball courts. Softball was extremely competitive and also drew a lot of fans. As the teams were leaving, I noticed one guy. He had a swagger I recognized. He hadn't changed much since he took my change and Coke fifteen years earlier. It was Billy. I watched him as he headed toward his team's dugout. His tee shirt still had rolled-up sleeves and there was a pack of cigarettes in one of the sleeves. Revenge swelled within me. I wanted to beat him as my father had beaten me. I moved closer to the exit. He was within fifteen feet.

"Billy."

He turned, looking to see who had called him.

"Billy. You are Billy from East 26th Street. Right?"

"Yeah," he said, smiling as if he was proud someone remembered him.

I was ready to introduce myself to him when he turned his back for a moment. When he did, he grabbed a baby stroller, wheeled it around, and began walking toward me. A young woman, whom I presumed to be his wife, was walking with him. She looked downtrodden as if she didn't want to be there.

Looking at me, Billy asked, "Do I know you?"

Billy didn't seem too big to me now. I had grown to be just over 6'5" and over 200 pounds, while Billy was about 5'8" and about 150 pounds. To think that he had towered over me so many years ago.

"Yeah, I think so. I'm Hughie McMahon."

"Hughie McMahon! Look at the size of you. Wow. I haven't seen you in years."

I looked at his wife and the baby in the stroller and knew. Billy's life was no bargain. I felt sorry for her, the baby, and for Billy. This was as good as it was going to get for them.

My anger was all gone. "Yeah, it's been a long time. Everything going okay with you?"

He gave me a half smile. "Pretty good."

"Take care; good seeing you," I turned and left. That was the last time I saw him. I believe God gave me an opportunity. I could have chosen the path of revenge or forgiveness. Fortunately, I chose the latter.

I jumped to score one day at practice in my senior year and came down hard on my left wrist. It was broken and remained in a cast for twelve weeks. I believed my basketball career ended with a thud, literally. It was one of those moments that reminded you that life is really unexpected. Nothing you can really do can change destiny and what is written for you. This, I suppose, was also one of those events. Even though it was painful, I still played with a broken wrist the entire season. Though I finished my senior year, I didn't have enough credits to graduate. The coach was gracious enough to pay for my classes until I graduated, but he couldn't pay for my room and board. I left the campus but remained in class. I got a job bartending to make ends meet. That decision to bartend was one that led me down a dark path. Too many parties, too many girls, too many drinks. It's a bad life for someone who's immature despite his age. I had no goals other than to have a good time and satisfy my physical desires. Bartenders are the stars of the saloons. Girls are drawn to them as they are to rock bands. This was my life, but it didn't come without a cost. Even a new sports car can get a flat. During this time, I made a horrible decision. I was dating a young lady I truly cared about. We became pregnant; not her but "we." The decision to terminate a pregnancy when you're young and stupid seems to be an easy decision. For a guy, you have that "got off the hook" feeling, but I can't imagine it's that way for the woman. More regrettably, I made the same decision a few years later while in Finland.

I gave up the bar life and was invited to the rookie camp for the Milwaukee Bucks of the NBA. I gave it my best, but this time the guys were much better athletes and players than I was. I took classes sparingly and finally graduated with a degree in Liberal Arts. Shortly thereafter, I received a call out of the blue from an attorney in Chicago asking me if I was interested in playing basketball over in Europe. I asked him one question: "When's the flight?" I went and played in Oulu, Finland. It was my speed, and I loved every minute of it. The people were wonderful, and I realized how fortunate I was to get to go to Europe and have the trip paid for in full. I was having the time of my life; playing basketball and getting paid to do it. I did meet a wonderful young woman there as well. She was a police officer who was studying to be a judge. She was the second girl with whom we got pregnant. Though she was a great girl, I knew I was leaving and that she, too, wasn't the "one." She definitely knew that too, deep down. If I could have the opportunity to ask for forgiveness from her, I'd do it in a heartbeat.

In Finland, God found me again, and the experience was painful because I was not leading a good and holy life. This happened through the Eucharist and also through a chance meeting with the devil, indirectly– or at least something like "the devil."

There wasn't a Catholic Church in Oulu, nor even a Catholic presence. The nearest Catholic Church was in Helsinki, nearly four hundred miles away. Most Finns are Lutheran. Though there were Lutheran Churches in Oulu, I couldn't attend. I did have an opportunity to go to Helsinki to play in an All-Star game. While there, I found the Catholic Church and did go to Mass. The Mass was in Finnish, but I knew what was happening and followed along as the Mass proceeded. I felt a bit guilty that I hadn't been at Mass in quite some time. It didn't deter me from receiving the Eucharist; something I now know I should not have done. I was not living a Catholic Christian life. Receiving the Eucharist was, therefore, tantamount to blasphemy.

Upon returning to Oulu, I had an experience I will never forget. Oulu had one movie theater which played foreign films every now and then. As I was walking by the theater, I noticed a new playbill in the window advertising a new movie. The Exorcist was coming to town. Now, I had heard of this movie in the States but chose not to see it. It came out in 1973. Knowing that it would be in English with Finnish subtitles, I decided to go to the theater. When it opened, I arrived at the box office to buy my ticket. I arrived early as I believed there would be a rush to see an American movie. I purchased my ticket, bought a soda and candy bar, and went into the theater. The seating capacity of the theater was about four hundred. I plunked myself down in the middle and waited for the seats to fill and the movie to start. Commercials began about twenty minutes afterwards. Once the movie began, I looked around to find that I was the only patron; yes, the only one in the theater. I watched the entire movie, and it scared the hell out of me.

I left the theater and went to a local bar and had a couple of shots of bourbon. The walk back to my apartment was eerily like the mood of the film. It was cold, rainy, and quite dark. When I got into my apartment, I closed and locked the door. I thought to myself: If the devil is going to find me, he's going to find me here, out in the middle of no place and all alone. I lit a candle I had and tried to sleep. I slept very little that night. I knew why I couldn't sleep. I looked at the life I had been leading for the past few years and it wasn't pretty. There was an expression used in Brooklyn when I was growing up and it came to mind. "From the gutter to me is not up." I was in the gutter. The devil seemed, for the first time in my life, to be real. I never really thought of the devil as I did of God. God was real, but the devil? Not so much. All that changed from watching that movie, The Exorcist.

Though I thoroughly enjoyed my time playing ball in Europe, I missed the United States. It wasn't easy to converse with people who didn't understand English though they did their best to speak it. So, after playing in an All-Star game in Tarare, France, I decided to go home. It was a bittersweet decision, but I always knew it was the right one.

(Jumping (l) to block a shot in Finland 1975)

I left Europe and came back to Brooklyn. Since I hadn't been home in a few years, I thought things would be better there. I was wrong. I got a job in Manhattan working for Pinkerton's, a security firm. When I had saved a few bucks, I moved out of the house for good into an apartment in Park Slope. The cord was finally severed.

1970's Big Changes in My Life

THE LIFE OF A single guy in New York in the 1970's was exhilarating. I had a job, had no real responsibilities, played basketball on several teams, and dated far too often. Foolishly, it was a time of partying. I worked at Pinkerton's for nearly three years and had had enough of it. I needed a real job at a real company. One of my accounts at Pinkerton's was AT&T. As luck would have it, after deciding to leave Pinkerton's, I was offered a job at AT&T as executive protection (bodyguard) to the Chairman of the Board, John D. deButts. I was as excited to get this job similar to when I was to get the call from the coach at Marquette. Finally, I was going to start a real career.

(AT&T Corporate Headquarters NYC)

AT&T headquarters was an amazing building. Located at 195 Broadway in lower Manhattan, it was the jewel of old-line corporate strength—formidable yet elegant. And here I was, working there! Amazing that it actually happened. I was immensely thankful. The hours were long but never uneventful, but that is part of the job. Mr. deButts was a great man, much like the building, formidable yet elegant himself. He would occasionally introduce me to people I'd only seen on TV; Henry Kissinger and Gerald Ford, to name a few. It was an incredible time in my life. I had new experiences, which I never really thought I would ever experience before moving here. Honestly, how could it get any better?

I continued to play on a few basketball teams, though I had to curtail the number due to my new job.

Did I deserve all of these good things that were happening to me? Outwardly I bluffed that I did, but inwardly I knew I was lucky or even perhaps blessed. No doubt God had His hand on me though I didn't realize it at the time. Though I was living the high life, I had these stings always drawing me back to Church, back to God. I didn't go every Sunday, but now and then, I would drop into daily Mass at St. Peter's Church on Barclay Street just around the corner from AT&T. When alone in Church, the scales of my pride fell away, and I was face to face with myself. I didn't like what I saw but wasn't strong enough to change once I left Mass.

I TURNED AROUND, AND THERE SHE WAS; THE ONE

One evening, one of the teams I played for in Brooklyn had a game in Manhattan. After the game, we went to a bar (Keats) on the East Side for a few beers. It was about 9:30 PM and there were only a few people at the bar. We went toward the back and ordered a few beers. When they came, I turned to look at the other customers. There were two girls at the bar: one standing, the other sitting. When I looked at the one standing, I felt as if I had been hit by a truck! There she was! The "one"! It wasn't just that she was stunningly beautiful. She was the "one" I had seen in my imagination ever since I was six years old. I was nearly paralyzed. You would think it only happens in movies, but no. There was I, completely stunned, speechless, and in awe of the woman I barely knew at the time.

I hadn't been shy to talk to a woman in years, but here I was, feeling like I was seventeen again. She turned and looked at me as if she knew I was looking at her. I decided to go over and talk. The closer I got, the more I knew. We began to chat.

"I'm Kathy." She also introduced me to her sister, who was with her at the bar.

After a few pleasantries, I asked where she worked. She said, "AT&T."

I was stunned.

"Really?" I responded, taken aback. It was a long time since anything had surprised me like this.

Now, AT&T was a huge corporation, at the time, the largest in the world. In Manhattan alone, there must have been twenty-five AT&T buildings. What are the odds I would run into the "one" and find that she worked at the same company? She said she worked downtown. I said I did as well. I said I worked at 195 Broadway. Her eyes popped as she said, "So do I!" When I told her what I did, I don't think she believed me right away, but after I proved it by mentioning a few names, she accepted that I was telling the truth. The more we talked, the more I knew. There was more to her than stunningly beautiful, good looks. She was real. She had a good heart and a sense of humor. She had something inside of her that I recognized as the same thing inside of me. It was that spark of life that I realized later was that part of God in her. It is in all of us, but we hide it. She said that she and her sister needed to go, and they left.

As she left, I thought she had no idea she was the "one." Everything about her, in those brief moments, confirmed it to me. It wasn't love at first sight since I had already seen her in my imagination for most of my life.

We went out several times. I was usually tongue tied and couldn't say what I wanted to say. She was the "one," but if I told her, perhaps she'd think I was nuts. I never tried anything physical with her as I wanted this to be the perfect relationship. I wanted her forever and I treated her like an angel. I couldn't do otherwise. Though I knew she was the "one" for me, she never gave me the impression that I was the "one" for her. I don't know if she was indifferent or just playing her cards close to her chest. I had never experienced this before. I could always talk and get others to talk, but she couldn't or didn't want to. Perhaps she was waiting for me to say something, but it never came out. A few minor things she said told me perhaps I wasn't the one for her though I couldn't put my finger on it. One evening we were going out to see a movie, and she asked if we could drop by her mom's home as she wanted to pick something up.

"Sure, no problem." I had never met her mother.

We arrived at her mom's home. "Come on in."

"Are you sure?"

"Yes, come on in."

We went in, and she said as she flew by her mom, "This is Hugh."

That was it. I stood there as if I was the paperboy awaiting payment. I sensed her mom was uncomfortable as well. Meeting someone's parents is a big deal, at least to me. It was only a few minutes but it seemed like an hour just standing there. Finally, Kathy came back.

"Bye mom," she said and waved, and we headed out the door.

I never brought it up, but it always made me feel as though I was just another date. I just didn't feel she had the feelings for me I wished she had.

While on a business trip to New Orleans with Mr. deButts and his wife, Trudy, he asked me to join them for lunch. I was surprised, but he insisted. As we were finishing, he asked, "Are you still seeing Kathy?"

I was floored. I should have known he would know what was going on in my life since he seemed to know everything that went on in the company.

"She doesn't really show any interest."

"Really?" He responded with a great deal of astonishment. "You may want to try again."

Mrs. deButts jumped in with her beautiful Tidewater Virginia accent. "Well, if she doesn't, I have a number of very lovely young women from very good families that I can introduce you to!"

Mr. deButts looked at his wife and smiled, and then looked at me. "Just call her."

When we got back to New York, I did, and we went out. But it was the same story. Nothing. It was as if she wanted to be somewhere else. Was this just a game? After seven dates, I stopped calling. It hurt like hell as I knew that she was the "one."

I went back to what I knew best, basketball. I continued to play and continued to work. The joy of playing and the joy of the job faded as I knew that Kathy was still in the same building and we would run into each other now and then. I found myself praying for her. Not praying to get together but rather praying that she would be happy and safe; that she would find someone special for her as I had found her, who was special to me. I began to realize, however, that there probably isn't just that "one" and only, and I'd better just get on with life.

The sexual revolution of the 1960's and 1970's gave license to young impressionable nitwits like me to delve into a foolish and devastating lifestyle. The song, "If You Can't Be with The One You Love, Love the One You're With." seemed to be the mantra of the day, and it was certainly mine. The term "free love" is anything but free—as I learned the hard way. There is no such thing as a free lunch. Every invoice must be paid. The hauntings and the guilt of so many evils I took part in overwhelmed me and brought me to my knees. Though forgiven, the abortions remain a reminder of a past that cannot be erased.

With the invention of the pill, many women felt liberated to experiment with sex and dove headlong into the arms of any guy available. Guys were more than willing to catch as many as they could. After all, there were no consequences. It was all fun and fun all the time. Though I was quite shy in the late 1960's, there were plenty of girls who weren't. None of us was innocent, and all of us lost our innocence.

Later in life, I realized that sex is different for a woman than it is for a man. Women, for the most part, look at sex as a commitment. Not so men. For us, it's mostly physical. Whether it's the feeling of conquest, power, or gratification, men don't think of commitment until they realize they don't want to be alone and truly need someone with whom they can share their life and share themselves.

Though I did my share of partying, at a certain point, I began to yearn for a deeper relationship and sense of home. I felt this yearning one night, for instance, when I stopped at a bar. I was on the way home from playing a basketball game on Long Island. It was around 1 AM. Farrell's bar was still open, so I decided to get a nightcap. When I walked in, I noticed three or four guys down at the end of the bar laughing it up and drinking. I knew these guys and knew that each was married and had young kids. I looked at them and said to myself, "I'd give anything to have a wife and kids, and here these guys are at the bar while their families are home." Looking into the mirror behind the bar, I said to myself, "At least they have someone; you're all alone." Not long afterwards, I decided, most foolishly, that I was going to marry the next good girl that I met. I didn't want to be alone, and I was now 30 years old.

I did just as I had decided. Being a guy of Irish descent, I thought the girls coming off the boat were all Maureen O'Hara. It is not the case. I met an Irish girl working in an Irish bar in lower Manhattan. I had begun working there as a riot control engineer, a bouncer. Again, too many drinks and loneliness (the sense of being alone) led to another pregnancy. I wasn't going to go through another abortion, so Rosemary and I married. It was a catastrophe. I knew two weeks before the wedding that it was going to be a long, long, long life. But I couldn't and wouldn't back out. Six months after we were married, Rosemary told me she hated sports! Talk about not knowing each other. The one thing that was my safety net, basketball, she hated. Besides the unwanted pregnancies (which led to abortions), my first marriage was the worst decision

I had ever made. No free lunches. The bill had to be paid. This was the first instalment. I had to pay for my foolishness by discontent. We had nothing in common, which is not a good sign for a lasting relationship.

We had four sons: Mike, Brendan, James, and Matthew, whom I love unconditionally, but my marriage to their mother was an utter calamity. The relationship I had always wanted had passed me by. The girl at AT&T was the "one," but that was long past, and I had to play the cards which I, myself, had dealt. Catholics don't divorce, especially Irish Catholics. You're better off dying than divorcing. You stay married because of the children. After all, if you divorce, you are going to Hell! After nine years, we divorced. I believe she wanted to remain married out of fear but not out of love.

During that first year of marriage, I continued to play basketball but only sparingly. One evening, we were playing in an old junior high school gym. We walked up a few flights to get to the gym. The old dark and dank place, smelling of years of sweat, looked as though it hadn't seen any life in years. Just before the game started, it hit me. I had lost my passion for playing. I didn't want to be there. My life was as dark as that gym. The thing that had sustained me for twenty years had died. I wanted to leave but didn't. I went through the motions of playing, but my heart wasn't in it. It was over, as was my life. I was just going to go through the motions of life until my life ended. My payment for foolishness: feeling dead.

It was January 23, 1978, when I began working at AT&T. I had made it, and finally arrived. That magnificent building at 195 Broadway in Manhattan, whenever I entered, gave me a sense of strength and wonder. The lobby, with its marble floors, granite columns, and alabaster chandeliers, was the definition of elegance, grandeur, and power. I was so full of myself I could have exploded.

(AT&T Lobby)

However, by July of that year, I realized how little I knew. Quite a number of the men working there had master's degrees in electrical engineering, and most of the women there had master's degrees in various disciplines. Just by observation, I was put in my place. I examined my pedigree and concluded that I knew three things and only three things. I knew basketball, I knew bartending, and I knew how-to pick-up women. It scared the hell out of me. Basically, I knew nothing compared to most of the people in headquarters.

Two weeks after this realization, I had the opportunity to back up to Marquette for a basketball reunion. I had the chance to speak with a Jesuit priest whom I'd known when I was playing. I confided in him regarding my lack of knowledge of anything of importance. The three things I did know, I shared with him.

He smiled and kindly said, "Do you know what that day was?"

"No." I shook my head.

"That was the first day of your education. When you admit to yourself that you don't know, you have reached a foundation. Do you know what the second day is?"

"No." I was again shaking my head.

"Doing something about it."

I thanked him and realized he was right. I had to do something about it. Not long afterward, AT&T began a program with Long Island University for Liberal Arts so that graduates could obtain a graduate certificate in business. I jumped at it. I studied like crazy. I put in effort for that goal equal to what I had given to basketball. I was successful and realized that I could learn. I wasn't just a jock. A few years later, AT&T partnered with the University of Pennsylvania's Wharton School of Business to have qualified employees participate in a Corporate MBA program. Again, I jumped at it, and again, I was successful.

The three things I had known earlier in my life were fleeting. Knowledge, true knowledge, is critical for making good decisions, the right decisions. I was proud of myself, but not with the kind of ego pride seen in actors and athletes. Instead, this was self-esteem, pride before God: the pride that comes from within and remains there. This education helped me tremendously in the positions I held at AT&T and afterward. All of this; these changes in life and attitude came after I chose God and not myself.

As you will discover in what follows, around this time, I experienced a life–changing revelation, which finally gave me the peace I had been seeking. My youngest brother died. The impact of his death brought me to question everything, including life itself. I had so wanted, for my entire life, to be loved, to be happy, to be at peace, but I was seeking something that couldn't be satisfied by another human being. It took the death of my brother for me to begin a journey I had never considered. The journey continues. I now know *Who* that *ONE* is, the "one" I had been trying to find all of my life. When I found Him, I received love, real love, and I was loved for who I really am. From then on, I've been happy to be really known, and I am at peace with that.

The Year Was 1986.
My Life Changed.

MY FIRST WIFE, ROSEMARY, was due to give birth to our twin sons, James, and Matthew, in late April of 1986. My aunt Kathleen told us in late 1985 that she would come down and spend time helping out once the twins were born. Everyone has a favorite aunt. Aunt Kathleen was mine. She was my mother's younger sister. She was smart, funny, caring, and one of the three people I knew who loved me. My other two favorite relatives were my grandmother and my brother Christopher. Kathleen was going to come to Dallas from New York right after the twins were born. My wife was thankful for the offer and anxious for Kathleen to arrive.

I came home from work on Tuesday, January 7th, 1986. Rosemary was sitting on the sofa and crying. She looked at me and said, "Your Aunt Kathleen died." The floor came out from under me. How could this happen? She was as healthy as could be. She had a broken hip that had been fixed, and she was about to be discharged from the hospital. An aneurysm. She died within minutes. I was devastated. I loved her and now she was gone. I flew up to New York for the funeral. I was numb. The sight of her in the casket was almost too much. She was sixty-nine years old. I remember going to the gravesite but nothing after that, not even how I got home.

My wife was disappointed and saddened as she liked my aunt. Having two small boys with two more on the way was daunting. I asked my wife's two sisters to come over from Ireland. They jumped at the chance. I told them this was a surprise gift for Rosemary and not to say anything. No one said a word. Rosemary was floored when her sisters, Rita and Agnes, walked through the door. They arrived shortly after James and Matthew were born and stayed for six weeks.

At the same time that we were expecting twins, one of my younger brothers, Stephen, and his wife, Debbie, were expecting twins. Tragically, their twins died a month after ours were born. They were premature: another crushing blow to the family. What do you say? How can you comfort? We had healthy sons, and they lost their daughters.

In September, my mother called to let me know that my Godmother, Aunt Rita, had died. She was one of the sisters of my father. She and my father, I believe, hated each other. I liked her. She was straightforward, honest, and never took any guff from my father. I didn't make it to her funeral, but always remembered her fondly. Death is always a tragic blow to the bubble we all live in. It reminds us that life is futile, short, and not ever-lasting. It also allows you to think about the afterlife. 1986 was a difficult year, with all this death and disappointment. I often used to think to myself, "Could it get worse?" Apparently, it always can.

If you haven't had that moment in your life, that crossroads, which required you to choose one path or another, you've either avoided or missed it entirely. Avoidance meant you knew the challenge had occurred, but you chose to send it packing or store it away for another day. Avoidance gnaws at you, and you send that moment deeper and farther away from your life. However, that challenge—that crisis — is still there.

If you missed the event entirely, you were not engaged in anything but yourself. Your clouded view of life itself sent that moment away, and it passed you as quickly as a falling leaf in a gust of wind—falling to the ground far away and disintegrating, all because of your hubris. Choosing yourself above all others, and all things, prevented you from seeing and experiencing that moment. Thankfully, there are other leaves that fall and perhaps, just perhaps, you'll notice them and take advantage of the next moments.

My moment came upon me when my youngest brother, Christopher, died. He was 28 years old. He passed away in his sleep from natural causes. That was the opinion of the doctors who performed the autopsy. How could this young, vibrant giant of a man pass away from natural causes? He was a great athlete, 6'8," 240 lbs., and about to get married. He had bought a house and received a nice promotion at work. His life was all before him, and in a moment, it was over. A second autopsy reiterated what the first said: natural causes.

(Christopher just before he died and our Uncle Tom)

Chris lived in Brooklyn with another brother, Patrick. Patrick called me in Dallas on Saturday, October 4th, 1986. He told me to sit down three times. I finally said I was sitting. He told me. I reeled in the chair, not believing what he said. How could I believe it? It was Christopher. He couldn't be dead. Patrick then said the words that made it real, "The police are here now." Then I knew. I knew for certain. I was crushed. I felt pressed to the earth. I sobbed uncontrollably as I loved him, loved him as any man could love a brother.

My plans to go up to Brooklyn remain a blur even now. The flight was on Sunday. I remember going to Mass in Dallas and crying through the entire Mass. I don't remember the flight at all. My best friend in New York, Mike Burke, picked me up and drove me to my older brother John's apartment in Manhattan. I got to the apartment around 6 PM. John's two young children went to stay with their aunt while I stayed with John and his wife. We had something to eat though I wasn't hungry. John was talking, but I wasn't listening. All I could do was sit there and think. Finally, around 2 AM Monday morning, I went to the kid's bedroom to sleep. It was a beautiful night, bright and crisp. I opened the windows and then sat on the bed. I sat for a few minutes. Then, for the first time in my life, I talked to God. Yes, I talked to Him.

Where else could I go? My life of 38 years, up until that point, was spent mostly on myself. Up until that point, I had, so I believed all the answers. I was seemingly content with life, or at least I was putting up with it, but there was something always gnawing at me. Was there more? Was there something I was missing? I was always asking myself these questions. But here I was, sitting at the edge of a bed, with no answers to any questions. So, I talked to God.

"I'm not going to ask You why this happened; only You know. You know why he was born, why he died. You know why any of us is born and why any of us die. I need to know; I really need to know the answer to one question, and then everything will make sense; his life, his death, everyone's life, everyone's death. My question," and I asked this as sincerely as I have asked any question in my life, "Is there an afterlife? I really don't know. I need to know."

I then lay down on the bed and drifted off to sleep. I woke up four hours later at 6 AM. I sat again on the side of the bed. Here I was, on the east side of Manhattan on a Monday morning with the windows wide open, and there wasn't a sound. There wasn't a horn, a siren, a bus, or a boat I could hear. It was as quiet as snowfall in a forest. Not a sound. I decided to get dressed and go for a walk.

As I got to the street, I sensed there were people around me, but I couldn't *feel* their presence. It was as if I had walked under one of those see-through umbrellas that young girls used. I was in a bubble as I walked. All I could think about was Chris. I walked west to 1st Avenue and turned south, and came to 19th street. I turned right on 19th street and kept walking on the south side of the street. I was midway down the block when it hit me.

(Christopher 1985)

From within my chest a voice, not audible to my ears, arose: "Relax, there is an afterlife. Just lead the life you're supposed to lead."

I was stunned, as if frozen in time. I questioned myself, "Did that really happen?" Perhaps because I questioned the reality of this *voice*, it came to me again more forcefully but not threateningly, "Hey, relax, don't worry about it! There *IS* an afterlife. Just lead the life that *you* are supposed to lead!" The second time the voice spoke, it was slower and emphasized the "you" powerfully.

I continued to walk in a daze over what had transpired, both Chris' death and the voice. I stopped walking and found myself in front of a Church, a Catholic Church. The bulletin board indicated that a Mass would begin in a few minutes. I went in. There were some older women in the front pews, but other than that, the Church was empty. One of the women turned to me and said they were praying the Rosary and to come and join them. I politely declined and sat in a pew near the rear. Mass was a blur, and I left in the same daze that had consumed me ever since Saturday.

I walked back to my brother's apartment. He let me in and asked, "Where did you go?"

"I went for a walk and wound up going to Mass."

"What Church?"

"It was on 2nd Avenue."

"That's our parish, Epiphany. Did you know that's the parish grandma was married in when she came here from Ireland?"

I had no idea. I didn't tell him about the voice, how God spoke to me in the middle of 19th Street, or how I talked to God. John wouldn't have believed me. I didn't tell anyone for several years. Strangely, I was no longer devastated that Christopher had died. I was still crushed by my loss but not for Christopher. He was in Heaven. Now, I understood because God had shown me the reality of the afterlife. He led an exemplary life; a life caring for and doing for others. Everyone loved him. Over a thousand people came to the wake. A few of them, whom I had never met, told me how much Christopher loved me and how proud he was of me. As we're Irish, we never say tender and emotional things to one another. Stubbornness, I guess, is the reason.

After the funeral, I flew back to Dallas. "Lead the life you're supposed to lead." This message kept coming at me. What was it? What was this life? I asked myself these questions repeatedly. I loved my four sons, loved them unconditionally. However, I didn't love their mom. I didn't love her before we married, but we married anyway. We should never have gotten married; she knew it as well, but. . .people make bad decisions.

So, what was the "life" I was supposed to lead? I realized, after much agony and pain, that I couldn't remain married and find this life. I had to choose. I chose God. He was my only choice. I had led a life not worthy of anyone. I bought into the life of my society and of many young men, at the time and at every time (I guess), a life of partying and chasing skirts. Oddly, while living this life, I could sense it was wrong, yet I continued living it.

It took my brother's death to bring me to my knees and bring me to the reality of life. Yes, there is an afterlife. I know this and know there are two choices: Heaven or Hell. I lived in Hell most of my life. I didn't want to live in it forever. The road back to God is not easy. There are overwhelming temptations. The ease of going back to the old life is always there, and there are hazards on the road ahead, which is strewn with broken glass and sharp rocks. As I was traveling this painful road, it dawned on me that I couldn't turn back. That old life was one of death and led to soul death as its destination.

Fatherhood

For three years, I agonized about divorce and leaving my sons. I moved to a small apartment a few miles from their home, but it felt as though I was on the other side of the world. Two steps forward and one step back was the journey. I was conflicted as to what to do. I was at my end. I had nowhere to go. The pain of hurting my sons, and their mom, was, at times, overwhelming. One night, as I knelt by my bed, I literally cried out to God and called Him "Father!" At that moment, my life changed. I got an immediate answer, "Yes, I am your Father. I told you to give Me everything, and I will take care of you."

Yes, I realized God is my Father, my Creator. I had to give everything to Him. That night I slept the entire night for the first time in years. I woke that next morning fully aware that I had to live that life that God had created me to live: to live for Him as my brother Chris had done.

It took two *moments* in my life to bring me to God, and I haven't looked back. The voice I heard on 19th Street and the voice I heard on my knees in the apartment were the same voice.

Searching, Praying, Trusting

ONE SUMMER, I TOOK the boys on a vacation. We piled into the car, and off we went. The first stop was a friend's home in Little Rock, AR. They had a pool, and the boys loved it. Next stop was Nags Head, NC. A friend of mine from college invited me out for a week on the beach with the boys. They never forgot it, and Brendan decided at that point that he wanted to live on the water. Surfing, crabbing, and fishing were a young boy's dreams; my boys were no exception. After Nags Head, we drove to Washington, D.C. and stayed with my mom's cousin for an evening. I took the boys around D.C. to show them the sights. They liked it but wanted to be back at the beach!

As I wanted them to see my family and where I grew up, we made it up to Brooklyn the next afternoon. My uncle and aunt graciously offered to put us up for a few days in their home in Greenwich, CT. It was a whirlwind trip and exhausting for me, but I loved it. Being with them and having fun were great gifts.

Prior to leaving, my father shook my hand and said, "This is for the boys." I didn't look at what he gave me but I knew it was cash. I just put it in my pocket. "Thanks."

It took two days to drive back from Brooklyn to Dallas. As we left Brooklyn and drove over the Verrazano Bridge, I sensed there might be something wrong with the car. It broke down on Staten Island. We spent six hours there waiting for the car to be repaired. In classical New York custom, the repair shop over-charged me and wouldn't take an out-of-state check; Texas plates, you know!

I was strapped for cash but remembered the cash my father had just given me. I thought it might help; perhaps he gave me a couple of hundred for the boys. I took the cash from my pocket. It was $800.00. I was stunned. The amount easily covered the extortion of the Staten Island prices. Again, God was working in my life and in my father's life as well.

The boys don't remember the breakdown, but they do remember that Staten Island smell; the landfill takes up most of the island! Not once during the entire four-thousand-mile trip did one of them say, "Are we there yet?" The entire trip was an adventure for all of us.

Now, the road hasn't been lined with roses and hymns since that time. There have been wonderful highs and gut-punching lows. However, through all of them, I have remained focused on God and His plan for me and for life itself. I recently heard a Bishop say, "*De profundis clamavi ad te Domine* (From the depths I cried out to you Lord)." I was at the depths, and I cried out. He answered me, and He'll answer you.

If you have questions as to why you're here and haven't figured it out, perhaps you, like me, can ask as I did, and receive your answer. There's no one answer too, I believe everyone has their own journey and path, but you can only know yours by talking to Him, opening up to Him, and most importantly, asking Him to guide you. And He will, He always does. All you have to do is wait.

My journey didn't come without pitfalls and temptations. Before my divorce was completed, I met a woman who had lost her mother about the time my brother had died. We became friends through consolation. The friendship grew. As it grew, I continued my search to "live the life I was created to live." We talked about many things, including faith. She wasn't Catholic and had little interest in the Church. She knew Catholicism was very important to me but thought it too demanding for her. This would be a road-block, but I hung on, hoping the situation would change. It doesn't, and it didn't.

Something she said stuck with me. She told me that I needed to keep everything in balance and that I was placing too much emphasis on God. How can anyone keep everything in balance when God isn't the center of your life? We were sitting at her desk the day she said this. There was a pencil holder containing a few pencils on her desk. I removed five of the pencils and lined them up in a row from left to right. Pointing to the pencils, I said, "Is this what you mean by having everything in balance? The first one is God, the second is family, the third work, the fourth is friends, and the fifth is play. Each is worth twenty percent?"

"Yes."

"If I do it that way, I will make all of them gods or diminish God for each of them!" I took the first pencil and placed it over the other four saying, "God has to be pre-eminent, and all other things are below Him." She just looked at me and shook her head. I knew then we were not walking the same path.

In the Spring of 1988, I was torn between divorcing and re-turning to my wife. I didn't love her, and if she was honest, she didn't love me. The woman I had met at work had become more than a friend but not yet an intimate one. Regrettably, that came later. Being intimate would have destroyed me, and nearly did. She was the antithesis of my first wife; very outgoing and filled with a zest for life. I couldn't go back to living a life in the flesh. Once again, I had to choose. I chose God to be first in my life. Though the woman wanted me to move in with her, I couldn't and settled on an apartment near my sons. Further, she wanted me but didn't want to be involved with my sons.

Anyone who says going through a divorce is painless is a liar. It is devastating to all parties. My decision to divorce was based on several factors. Primarily, I should never have married the mother of my sons since there was no real love there from the beginning. Leaving my sons was the most difficult thing I have ever done. Though I wasn't deserting them, I would not be with them, and that left me questioning everything. The woman I was seeing of-fered me some qualities I'd missed with my first wife of nine years: I could talk to her, confide in her, and be comfortable around her. I was ripped apart inside as to what to do. Would suicide be better? I asked myself more than once. I had made so many bad and foolish decisions in my life. Was I about to make another one? A final one? Again, no free lunch. I was handed another bill I had to pay. I was flailing about with seemingly nowhere to turn.

When I transferred to Texas, I became a Corporate Investiga-tor with AT&T. One afternoon at work, I was scheduled to inter-view a witness for a case. My personal problems were impacting my job. I was a wreck. All I could think of was my sons, the other woman, and my wife. My head was exploding, and I couldn't con-centrate. I didn't want to hurt anyone, yet I was hurting everyone. My boss came to me and told me my witness had arrived and was in the conference room. I looked at my boss in a panic. "I can't do this." She was stunned but saw the look on my face and said she would take the case.

When she left the room, she closed the door. Here I was, standing in my office with no solution, nowhere to go, no life. As I stood next to the floor-to-ceiling window on the tenth floor of our building, I looked down at the pavement below. It ran through my mind that it would probably be better for everyone if I just ended it all. I stood there with that thought for some time. Suddenly, a visual came to me and an insight: a scene of my four sons, standing together talking, twenty years into the future. One of them said, "You mean the old man killed himself because he loved someone who wasn't our mom? Didn't he love us enough to stick around?" With that, I backed away and never considered suicide again. No matter what it took, I would be there for my sons.

God certainly placed this thought, this visual, before me so that I could glimpse what life would be like for my sons without me. Now, it hasn't been all wine and roses between us since I di-vorced their mother. We—my sons and I—are still in each other's lives, although at times estranged. No doubt the divorce took a toll on them. Only later in life did one of them tell me he had felt abandoned by me. No assurances from me could alter this belief, and perhaps the others also felt abandoned. Horrible events took place of which I had no knowledge until much later. These hard times only solidified their conviction that I had not been there for them. If I had stayed, would their lives have been easier? If I had stayed, my life would have been harder, for I would not have become who I am. I keep avenues open and bridges intact with the prayerful hope of complete reconciliation. I'll do so until my final breath. Yes, divorce is hard; it's crushing but sometimes necessary.

Moments of Grace

Once I parted company with the woman at work, I decided to take time off from the world. I needed to learn more about myself, who I really am, who I used to be, and especially who I wanted to become. I began going to a Church, St. Rita's, near my office. It was, at the time, a Jesuit parish. There was a daily Mass at 5:30 PM. I was going nearly every day, seeking, questioning, pleading, and wondering. At the back of the Church, there was a small alcove with a crucifix. Often, people would go and knee before the crucifix and pray. I had done so a few times, seeking guidance. One evening, I went there to pray. In front of me was a young Hispanic man praying. I asked Jesus to grant him his prayer as I recognized in this young man a desperation similar to mine. Perhaps, just perhaps, God would answer his prayer. When he got up and left, I went to the kneeler and knelt. As I was going to kneel, I sensed that someone had come behind me. I didn't want to spend too much time there as this person might need help more than me. I quickly prayed and got up. As I was passing, this person, an older woman, gently grabbed my arm. I thought she might have needed some help.

"Yes?"

"I don't know who you are, but I pray for you every day."

I looked at her and lost it. I began sobbing uncontrollably.

"Just keep coming and praying. God will answer you, and you will be fine." She squeezed my arm and looked so lovingly into my eyes. I didn't know what to say.

"Thank you," I said as I turned and left. I had no idea that anyone had noticed me. I always sat at the back of the Church during Masses, as any good Catholic does, and never for a moment thought that anyone would be praying for me, especially someone I didn't know. It surprised me that anyone would care for me or look at me with such empathy and care. I didn't think I was that important to anyone.

The woman, Marion Leahy, became a dear friend over the next twelve years. She was a wonderful woman, full of life and love. One of a kind truly, the type of friend you only meet once in a lifetime. She was an "Auntie Mame" if ever there was one. She didn't take herself too seriously, yet took others seriously, especially those in need. She became a surrogate grandmother to my sons and called herself "Mother Inferior." As I got to know her, I realized we had several things in common. We were New Yorkers, and she reveled in finding one in me! She shared some of her life experiences with me as I did with her. Confiding in someone you trust brings amazing comfort.

Once I made the decision to search for that life God had created me to lead, the temptation to go back to the old life intensified. To combat your weaknesses—in my case, lust—is a daunting and constant battle. I've learned that growth and progress are never linear, as different factors can always tempt you to go back to your old ways. The Dallas/Ft. Worth area is filled with an abundance of strikingly beautiful women. They are in workplaces, restaurants, bars, and churches. The ratio of females to males in the area was decidedly in favor of males at the time, and the women were never shy about approaching any male. However, my goals were different this time, and I was more focused on myself spiritually. I continued to work but ceased dating. I didn't miss it. Getting to know myself was a great and necessary journey. I looked at myself for who I was and where I was in life. If I kept God as the center of my life, I would be anchored in truth.

Quiet introspection may help you or crush you. Being open to God's mercy and guidance is critical for moving onward. I did this. If I hadn't, I would have been mired in self-pity and eventually bitterness. It took the better part of a year to see all of the demons that plagued my life. Though I had done many bad things, I wasn't one of the bad guys and never wanted to be one of them. I loved my sons and wanted to be the dad I had always wanted to be. I could be alone and be happy. I liked myself and if others did, that was great. If others didn't, that was great as well since it validated me. I knew I was being true to who I was and didn't need approval from others as to who I was. It was exhilarating and freeing. I was free to give myself to someone if I so chose and free not to as well. I was leaving it all to God as I had this new life. My focus in life was God first, my sons second, and everything else from there.

One evening, a few months later, I was watching a show on cable television. There was a nun in a brown habit speaking with people who were calling on the phone. One of the callers was a woman who had had an abortion. I could tell by the trembling in her voice she was devastated by her decision and wanted forgiveness. The nun spoke quite gently to her. Her next words numbed me. "Have you named your baby?" There was silence for a moment, and then the woman said, "No." The nun said, "Name your baby. She is a real person and is awaiting you in Heaven; so give your baby a name." The nun was Mother Angelica, who began the EWTN network. The weight of my decision to end the lives of my two children by abortion was overwhelming. Since the first one was a boy, I named him Paul. The second I named Charles. I think of them often and have asked for their forgiveness. I pray to meet them in Heaven.

I lived in that apartment for nearly four years. During those years, I was the dad to my sons I always wanted to be. It was a struggle financially, but we were happy. The boys said more than once that the time in the apartment was the best time in their lives. They would come over every Wednesday and spend the night as well as every other weekend. Rather than pizza and takeout, I cooked dinners and we ate together. I invited Marion over for dinner one evening, and she was stunned I was cooking! We had a roast, mashed potatoes, vegetables, and dessert. "And he cooks too!" she said with a laugh.

Good Priests Can Really Help

ALL THROUGH GRADE SCHOOL, high school, and college, I thought a priest was a priest. Sure, I had heard of Jesuits, Maryknoll's, and a few other orders, but I never understood the difference between them and the priests in regular parishes. Even when I went to Marquette, a Jesuit university, I didn't see any difference; they all dressed in black, just as local parish priests did.

I began attending daily Mass at St. Rita parish in Dallas in 1987 at the suggestion of a friend. He knew I had gone to Marquette and told me that St. Rita's was a Jesuit parish. Though still not fully realizing what it meant to be Jesuit, I chose to go for convenience since the Church was just around the corner from my workplace. There, I began to listen to the sermons. They were thoughtful, relevant, timely, and most important to me: sincere. Furthermore, the priests never read their sermons. None of them, not once. I learned Jesuits are highly educated; all have advanced degrees and many doctorates in various fields. Some are professors in universities, some engineers, and other physicians. Their fields run the entire gamut of educational areas and professions, yet they are also men of service. As their motto says, "Men for Others."

I was going through my own personal hell of separation and divorce; I needed to talk and decide on one of these Jesuits. One morning after Mass in 1988, I approached the young priest, Fr. Lawrence.

"How can I help?" was the first thing he asked. Not, "What's the problem?" but "How can I help?" I took him at his word.

While I explained my situation, he listened attentively for fifteen minutes or so.

"I understand."

With that, I was hoping he would give me a solution, an answer.

I told him I thought I needed to go on a retreat, purchased a Bible, and began reading it.

"Whoa, whoa, whoa! You are not ready for either and they would do you more harm than good if you did either or both now. What you need to do is find a good Catholic psychologist or counselor to help you navigate through all your issues." He said this passionately and lovingly.

"Once you have completed addressing your issues and finding answers, then and only then should you go on a retreat and begin reading the Bible. Right now, you don't have the understanding to read and comprehend what the Bible says or what it even is." Again, he said that with such care. This advice was how he could help me, true to his first question.

"I know two psychologists here in the parish, and I can give you their names if you like."

I thanked him as he wrote down the names. As I left, I realized he was right. I knew nothing about the Bible and nothing about retreats. What I did know was that I was a mess and needed help. I chose one of the two names on the paper and called for an appointment.

I had believed that anyone going to see a psychologist or psychiatrist was automatically nuts. I figured they thought you were nuts as well. Boy, was I wrong. I think this mindset is ingrained in people's thoughts, as visiting a doctor normally implies that there's something wrong with the patient. And why would anyone visit a doctor otherwise? It's only when it's your turn to seek help, you might understand; it's not really a sickness, not always at least. Sometimes you just need someone else to talk to and help you figure out life. Going to the doctor was one of the best decisions I made after many poor ones. The doctor I met was delightful, thoughtful, and patient, a kind man. He put me at ease immediately.

"Everyone has at least one issue, most people have more than one, even psychologists!" He made me feel as though I could let it all out, and over the period of nine months, I did just that. I didn't feel like an alien during our sessions, just a normal human.

After completing my sessions, I had a different view of life and myself. I realized I could make rational decisions. In the past, I would make many decisions based on the expectations of others (or what I perceived to be those expectations) rather than based on my own desires and expectations. That changed, not overnight but gradually. As I changed, my confidence grew. Yes, I made decisions about my life and for my sons. I learned to be the father I always wanted to be. I became that man.

In 1990, I finally did go on a retreat. I was ready by then. I went to the Jesuit retreat house in Lake Dallas, Montserrat. I learned much about God from conversations with these Jesuits and by now, slowly, I was reading the Bible. I had more questions than answers, but that didn't deter me from searching. Jesuit retreats are quite different from other retreats. They are silent retreats; you don't talk. For three and a half days, you are silent. Now, if you need to talk to a priest or go to Confession, you can do that, but otherwise you are silent. Silence is quite powerful, especially when you haven't ever been silent your entire life.

The retreat director gives you instructions when you arrive and encourages you to take full advantage of the silence and the grounds of the retreat house. There is a beautiful lake, wonderful walking paths, quiet glens, and comfortable chairs individually spaced throughout. There is a calming peace when you are all alone and alone with God. There are no distractions or temptations, just a stillness in the air, which you admire and use to speak to God and be only with him. When people say embracing stillness serves as the ideal path to establishing a spiritual connection with God. I think they are correct.

When I arrived there were thirty or so other men there, none of whom I knew. The instructions from the director included something inviting. At the back of the primary chapel was a smaller individual chapel accommodating only one retreatant at a time. Shortly after the noon meal on Saturday, I went to this chapel.

I entered and found a chair, a kneeler, a tabernacle, and a lit candle. After sitting for about 30 seconds, I realized I was there *ALONE*—with God. I immediately knelt. The longer I knelt, the smaller I got until I felt almost infinitesimal. Here I was, a street kid from Brooklyn, kneeling before God. The feeling overwhelmed me. I continued feeling smaller and smaller. Then, suddenly, it was different. I felt like I was supposed to be there doing what I was doing. I realized then, that someday, I *WILL* kneel before God and it would be better that I do it right then, rather than at the Judgment after death. I stayed for about 25 minutes. Spending time with God in that small chapel changed me. Spending time with God will do that.

At this time in my life, God would become the center. God basically said to me, "My way or yours?" I chose His. One word of caution. When you give your life to God, he will use you, though not abuse you. Not long after I made this commitment, an interesting event took place.

Priorities

There was a knock on my office door one afternoon. Johnny, one of the young men working for me, asked if he could come in and talk. I waved him in and he sat down. It wasn't formal so I asked, "What's up?"

He immediately responded by asking, "How do I get to be where you are? You know, manage this place and make your kind of money?" I thought to myself, You need to raise your sights!

"Well," I asked, "do you have a college degree?"

"No, but I'm thinking about going back."

"Good, but it's not critical for success." I was interested in why he wanted to have "my job." "Johnny, what's the most important thing to you in your life?"

"Money!" he said with such velocity and volume—and veracity—that it pushed me back into my chair.

Wow, I thought, his answer was almost frighteningly self-assured, but he was being honest.

I asked him how old he was. He said 23. I then asked him a question that started me on a journey I never, in my wildest dreams, thought I would be taking then or ever. I asked, "What's next after money?"

He looked a bit puzzled as if to say, "What do you mean 'what's next?'"

"After money, what is the next most important thing in your life?" I prompted.

He paused for a few seconds. "I suppose my family."

"Good," I asked him if I could write a few things down while we talked. He said, "Sure."

I took out a pad and wrote 23 years old on the top line and underneath this list:

Money

Family

Then I asked Johnny, "And then? What's next?"

Now he looked completely perplexed as if to say, What could be more important than money and family?

"What about your things, your stuff?"

"Oh yeah," he replied. "My truck, my new guitar; yeah, my things!"

"Then what?"

It was at this point that he was completely flummoxed.

"Do you have any friends?"

A lightbulb came on. "Yes, my friends."

I wrote this list down in order:

1. Money

2. Family

3. Things

4. Friends

He agreed that was the order. I then asked him, "What do you think will be the most important thing to you when you're 45 years old?"

He responded, "My family, definitely my family. My wife, my kids; definitely number one."

"And then?"

"Well, I'm going to need money, so money," he said. "Then my things, then friends," he finished.

I went on asking him about his list through the years until he was 65 years old.

He said, "Well, I'll be retired by then, and so, definitely my family is number one. My wife, kids, my grandkids. Then I suppose I'll have enough money, so my things will be next. You know, a lake house, a bass boat, my guitars. Then money, I'm going to need some money," he said as he laughed. "Then, my friends."

I listed all his responses and asked if I could run through them. He said, "Go for it!"

So, I went over them:

AGE 23 –

1. Money

2. Family

3. Things

4. Friends

Age 45 –

1. Family

2. Money

3. Things

4. Friends

Age 65 –

1. Family

2. Things

3. Money

4. Friends

He agreed that this was the order at each age and that he was happy with it.

I then asked him, "Johnny, what do you think or believe will be the most important thing to you on the day you're dying?"

He was taken aback by this just as I was taken aback by his first response about money. He thought for a few moments, slumped a little in the chair. He put his head down and pointed up. While he was pointing up, he said, "God," almost in a whisper.

"Johnny, when are you going to die?"

He shook his head, got up, and said, "I hate coming in here talking with you!" He was laughing a bit as he left.

As I did this exercise with Johnny, it wasn't my ideas that were guiding this conversation but a spiritual impulse. We all have priorities and believe, at any given time, they are the most important thing in our life and world. Our priorities usually change during our lifetimes, as did Johnny's. We, however, will leave this life behind; every single one of us. The question we avoid is: When?

This "When?" and probably also "Where?" should enter into the equation as we decide our priorities. I've shared this exercise over the years with several people, and many remember it as they speak of it now and then. So, will you also think about your list?

Walls

AFTER MY MEETING WITH Johnny, I realized I had to make amends. If I could, I'd reach out to those people I'd hurt and ask for forgiveness. A few weeks went by after I made this decision. One afternoon my phone rang. When the woman began to talk, I knew immediately who it was. The sound of her voice I had not forgotten. I said her name.

"How did you know it was me?"

"I could never forget your voice."

We talked and caught up. She was married and happy. I told her of my divorce and four sons. I knew I had to ask her to forgive me for how I'd treated her. We had gotten pregnant and decided upon an abortion. It was difficult to ask her for forgiveness as she might not give it. I knew I had to ask, and I did. She was so kind, so understanding.

"Of course, I forgive you. We were both too young and too immature."

"Thank you" was all I could say. I was choked up.

I was more than relieved. To seek and get forgiveness is life-affirming and life-giving. Reconciliation is cleansing. It gives you great parts of your life back. After she reached out to me to catch up, I decided to reach out to others, hopefully without infringing on their lives, to ask for forgiveness. All were gracious, kind, and understanding, and all were forgiving. Yes, reconciliation is a wonderful gift.

Reconciling with your past is the only way to grow. Don't be fooled. Without reconciling your life, you've missed the boat, missed the true cathartic medicine you need for life itself. It takes more than courage; it takes a self-awareness that few are willing to explore. To face your demons boldly is the only way to overcome them.

As I have related through this book, my early childhood was for me a struggle. Loneliness is one thing, but the profound sense of being alone is another. I built walls, and so do many others when they feel very alone. The wall first built is for protection. The next wall is a barrier of exclusion. The final wall is built of hardened steel that no one can penetrate, no matter how hard they try or how well-meaning their intentions. These walls, which I built for protection, isolated me. To build walls, I now realize, is the worst thing to do.

I believed I was building walls outwardly. The first was close to me, the second further out to exclude specific people, and the third further out, again, to keep away everyone else. All the remaining people would be kept at arm's length if they tried to gain access to me. This is the foolish assumption of those who choose to build walls. The walls don't go outward, actually; they go inward. After the first wall, the next is built inside of the first. The next wall, again, is built inside of that one until the builder (in this case, me) has built a fortress of walls. This fortress doesn't so much keep people out; instead, it keeps me in and suffocates me. I've built a fortress, in fact, a maximum-security prison.

Once I realized how this fortress isolated me, I felt a great relief. What a revelation. Only I could break down these walls. The only way I could was by self-actualization and self-acceptance. This acceptance gave rise to self-awareness. I looked at my entire life. Many times in my life, I had not been the person I wanted to be, and I had to reconcile myself to the person I actually was. This meant reconciling with others, too.

Modern technology afforded me the ability to search out several people in my life to tell them how sorry I was. My actions spoke along with my words. More than that, I asked each one of them for forgiveness. To say "I'm sorry" only got me off the hook, but asking for forgiveness, with the possibility of rejection, is a true form of penance. Incredibly, every single person forgave me. I was overwhelmed by their charity, their understanding, and their humanity.

Forgiveness reminds us of the immense strength of love within our lives and relationships. However, it's crucial to sincerely apologize and take steps to mend things. Keep in mind, the journey of healing hearts and rebuilding connections isn't simple. Yet, if you stay honest with yourself and committed to change, forgiveness becomes a transformative tool for personal growth. It's more than just saying three words; your actions need to reflect the change you seek.

Perfect Together

A FEW YEARS AFTER I met Marion, the woman at the back of the Church, I met Bonnie. We were introduced by Bonnie's brother, Ted, who was a fellow parishioner from church and a golf buddy. It took me a while to call Bonnie for a date as I was on my sabbatical from dating. My forty-fourth birthday was approaching as well as my fifteenth anniversary with AT&T. I was at peace with myself and just wanted to go out on a date. I hadn't anyone in mind until I remembered that Ted had suggested I call his sister. I did, and we went out. I was going to be me, the real me. If she liked me, fine. If not, that was fine as well. I didn't want to be a phony any longer. If she had a good time, great. If not, I couldn't help it. I just wanted a nice evening on a date. I had a wonderful time; a fun time being myself.

We almost didn't have that first date. Bonnie had given me her address. It was in Las Colinas, a suburb of Dallas. I wasn't familiar with the area and drove around looking for her apartment. I was running late, very late, and decided to call her. Rather than asking, "Where are you?" with agitation, she laughed with ease. "I'm on the other side of the highway!"

I finally made it, and we went out. The first stop was dinner at a wonderful Chinese restaurant. I didn't ask where she'd like to go. I wanted Chinese food!

"I love Chinese food," she blurted out as we went inside.

I kept telling myself, "Just be yourself, no matter what." Dinner was great and I was having a wonderful time. I mentioned to Bonnie that I had made plans to see a few Marquette friends downtown at an Irish pub and asked if she'd be interested.

"I'd love to," and off we went.

We arrived around ten o'clock. I introduced Bonnie and we had a few drinks with my friends. After a while, they had all left and we went to the bar for a nightcap. We talked and laughed and found we had a lot in common. The night flew by. It went so fast that the bartender said, "Hey, are you two staying all night?" I looked around and all of the chairs were on the tables and barstools on the bar, and no one was in the restaurant. It was two o'clock! We laughed and left. Time flies when you're engaged in a conversation with someone who truly understands you. It's wonderful how connections can create that effect.

After the date ended, I took Bonnie home, gave her a small kiss, and left. I had a great date! I wasn't sure if I was going to call her again soon, but she knew. I called the next Tuesday.

Bonnie, it turned out, had been on her own journey. She realized sooner than I had that God was putting us together. We dated a few times, and I met her mom and sister at church. They were a bit wary, it seemed, as I would have my sons with me every other Sunday. I suspect they thought Bonnie would be getting in over her head.

I told Marion that I was seeing a girl from St. Rita and asked if she would like to meet her. "Of course," she said laughingly as if she wanted to check Bonnie out. I often spoke of Marion to Bonnie, and she was anxious to meet her. I picked Bonnie up, and we went for dinner. Marion was waiting at the restaurant. Bonnie was quite nervous since she hoped Marion would like her. We had a great dinner and talked about many things. Prior to dessert, Bonnie excused herself and went to the restroom.

"I like her. She's the one."

I smiled. I didn't tell Bonnie for a month or so, though she asked! Both of us knew, and know, we aren't perfect, and the other isn't perfect, but we are perfect together. We've been married for 29 years, and though there have been lots of bumps in the road, we get through them because we know *the ONE* who gets us through them.

85

At My Father's Death Bed

As I was becoming the real me, the me I've wanted to be all my life, it was time to reconcile with my father. How could I approach him? Since I lived 1,500 miles away, there wasn't an easy opportunity to talk face to face. Never doubt the power of God. My job as an investigator in Texas rarely afforded me travel outside of Texas and a few neighboring states. My position, however, led me to where the evidence pointed. I was informed of a gambling operation within the company here in Texas. Diving deeply into it, I found out that numerous employees were involved in New Jersey. The case was big enough for my boss to send me there.

As I was flying up, I decided to go to Brooklyn, if I could, and see my father. He didn't really expect this, but I had to try reconciling with him.

As the case was winding down, I drove over to Brooklyn. My father had just come out of the hospital two days before my arrival. He had cancer and the doctors had removed a leg, hip, and some ribs (which were riddled with cancer). My mother, herself, was in the hospital having suffered two massive strokes. I went to see her first. It was gut-wrenching. I stayed a few hours and then visited my father.

One of my younger brothers, Patrick, and my sister were helping him out as much as they could. I arrived at the front door and took a deep breath. He knew that I was coming. How would he react? I came in and exchanged pleasantries with my siblings. We were not a very warm family. I said hi to my dad and sat down.

When they don't want to talk, the Irish are good at one thing: utter silence.

Patrick broke the silence by announcing a trip to the drugstore to get our father's prescriptions. My sister left to start dinner and asked if I would be staying. I claimed I had a meeting in New Jersey and couldn't attend.

So there we were; my father and I, in a room, alone.

"Dad, I'd like to talk to you, and I'd like to say something. Would you give me five minutes to talk, and then you can say whatever you want? Will you do that?"

He nodded affirmatively but said nothing. He had no idea what I was about to say.

"Dad, I hated growing up in our house. I hated the beatings, the yelling, the fights, and being thrown out. I know you are upset that I've gotten divorced, as you think I should have stayed no matter what. I couldn't. I didn't want to become someone I promised myself I would never be."

I tried to gauge his reaction. There was none. He just sat there, listening. Was he getting what I was trying to say? I continued, "I want you to know that I love my sons. I tell them I love them, and they tell me they love me. I'm okay with God too. And I want to tell you that I love you and though I know you can't say it, I know you love me."

He just sat there looking at me. Did he understand what I was saying, or as he had said to me all too often, "It's like I'm talking to a brick wall?" He then smiled and nodded his head yes. He didn't say it, but I knew what he meant. To see him smile, understand, and "get it" meant everything to me. This moment was like the moment in my brother's apartment when I spoke to God for the first time in my life. This was the very first time I really spoke with my father.

All the hate that had welled up in me for all of those years was gone. I realized then that he never had love in his life. His father probably behaved toward him as he did toward me and felt similarly. In my heart, I forgave him. I left a few minutes later.

My father died about three months later. I look back on those minutes I shared with him and thank God, truly, for the opportunity to set things right. At his funeral, I spoke about our relationship, not the gory details, just the intense friction. I then spoke of our last meeting and how all the tensions, dislikes, and even hatred dissipated. I was probably the last person to tell him that he was loved and probably the only person in more than fifty years to have said it to him directly, in his presence.

During the eulogy, I left everyone with this. Reconcile with everyone with whom you have a grievance. Once they are dead, you won't have the opportunity, and you will regret it.

God loves everyone, no matter who they are, no matter what they've done. So should we.

A Second Chance

Even though I gave my life to God, there were still challenges and tests. Rough times come for everyone. One rough time in my life occurred in 1996 when I was offered a great job outside of AT&T. I had met a man at church through a mutual friend. This man, who was the principal of a startup, was putting together a venture involving a few local businesspeople. The business was dedicated to sharing a great deal of its profits with charitable institutions throughout Dallas and Texas. After speaking with him several times, I felt that God was leading me to work with him. He went over the business plan, which was quite formidable, and his vision. He offered me a position as the head of security for the entire company at a salary three times greater than what I was making at AT&T. My sons were now living with us, and everything seemed to be working out fine. I took the leap and left AT&T for this new path, this new chapter, this new adventure. If it sounds too good to be true, you had better believe it.

I don't know the reasoning behind it nor his optimism, but the promised funding never came through. He hadn't told me there was no funding when I began, and I never received a paycheck. I wasn't alone. More than a few others had also been promised wonderful positions only to have their dreams smashed. I prayed daily, and sincerely, that I was on the right path. God wouldn't abandon me, and I wouldn't abandon Him. Several months went by, thirteen to be exact, and I had depleted my savings account to keep us afloat. Bonnie was praying as well but not complaining. She, too, trusted in God and believed everything would be fine. I finally had had enough and left this dream, this scam, and sought a reliable job. I reasoned that if I could get back into AT&T somehow, I could work my way back after a few years to the position I had once attained. Once I made this decision, I looked for positions in AT&T and Lucent Technologies. Lucent was, at the time, an offshoot of AT&T. I applied for a position at Lucent to work in the factory here in Dallas at $7.10 an hour. I got the job. Getting in was all that mattered. I trusted that God had a plan.

I was there working the second shift (4 PM to midnight), on a stamping machine. It was tedious work, to say the least, but I didn't complain. I was doing something and working toward something better; no matter what it was. Then, by happenstance, my old boss at AT&T, Larry, had heard I was working in the factory. We had worked on a couple of investigations there and still had some contacts. One mentioned to him that he saw me working there. Larry called me at home one day and asked if I'd like to grab lunch. During lunch, I told him all that had happened. He couldn't believe that the job opportunity had been a scam and couldn't believe that I had hung on so long.

Two weeks after our lunch, Larry asked if I'd be willing to do contract work for AT&T as an investigator. I began working the next week. I continued working at the factory as I was now receiving medical benefits. I arrived at Larry's office one morning around nine o'clock. He asked me to sit for a moment. He picked up his phone and called his boss out in California. His boss, Chuck, asked if I'd like my old job back. I was floored.

"Really?"

"Yes, if you're willing to come back, we'd like to have you."

"Yes, yes, I'd love to come back."

"Ok then, call Mike in New Jersey. He wants to talk with you." Mike was the Director of Corporate Security for all of AT&T. I had known Mike for twenty years.

I went to an outer office and called Mike. As I dialed, I told myself that I'd take the job no matter the pay, even at entry level.

He answered his phone.

"Mike, it's Hughie." Not knowing how he'd react, I chose to be informal.

"Hughie, how the hell are you? Coming back?"

"Yes, if you'll have me."

"Absolutely. When can you start?"

"How does tomorrow sound?"

"You'll need to resign from Lucent. Once you do, you can start. How's that?"

"Sounds great."

"Hughie, what was your salary when you left?" I told him and he said, "No problem, we can do that."

"Thanks Mike" was all I could say. That was it. I was back. I was starting at the beginning, but I was back. I called Bonnie and told her the news. God is certainly good when you trust Him. Perhaps God was testing me. I don't know, but what I do know is that I placed my trust in Him when everything around me was crumbling. And God came through.

My friend, Marion Leahy, passed away in February of 2001. Her son, Tom, asked if I would speak at her funeral Mass. I was humbled and honored to do this. It was hard to begin as the thought of our first encounter flooded my mind. I spoke of the loving friendship we had, though we were a generation in age apart. True friendship bridges those gaps. I quoted from the Book of Sirach during my brief talk. The reading describes true friendship.

From Sirach, Chapter 6, verses 14–17:[1]

> "A faithful friend is a sturdy shelter; he who finds one finds a treasure
> A faithful friend is beyond price, no sum can balance his worth
> A faithful friend is a life-saving remedy, such as he who fears God finds;
> For he who fears God behaves accordingly, and his friend will be like himself."

1. Saint Joseph Edition of The New American Bible

I look back on my college days and regret that I didn't understand Theology. Perhaps I would have majored in it if I had. I do now, however, rely on God's timing.

Though I could never go back to my old life, opportunities to help others present themselves. These events, which I'm about to recount, have all really happened, and some happened recently. I share them not to pat myself on the back, but rather to show that God will use you for good if you open your life and heart to Him. Let's help each other get home to Heaven by loving one another and by speaking plainly about the faith as Jesus and the Apostles did. Finally, I caution you; when you give your life to God, He'll use you! Be bold!

Love Letters

AFTER CHRISTOPHER DIED, I began to go to daily Mass. The experience I had on 19th Street in Manhattan drove me to find what I was supposed to do, and who was I supposed to be. While going to Mass, I listened attentively to the prayers and the readings. The prayers I understood but not the readings. On February 23, 1988, I decided to buy a Bible. I had no idea there were different kinds of Catholic Bibles. I settled on the Saint Joseph Edition of the New American Bible.

I began following along in the Bible, with the readings for the daily and Sunday Masses. Now, I'm not judging those who read, but I didn't think many comprehended what they were reading. Many, in my opinion, read words, and though they read solemnly, they lack understanding. Rather than just complaining about it, I became a lector. I felt I was called to do this.

It's daunting, when you really think about it, to get up in front of a congregation and read the Word of God. From the first day I read until now, I say a prayer to the Holy Spirit that the Word may be received and understood by those to whom I read. I pray that my reading is never about me, for it isn't. It's critical to know the original setting of the Word, when it was written, by and for whom, the circumstances involved, and the original audiences to which the Word was first proclaimed.

As a lector at St. Rita parish in Dallas, I read quite often. One duty of the lector on Sunday was to welcome people to Mass. I had done this for a few years and noticed that so many Catholics seem to be attending Mass just to check off the boxes and indicate that they fulfilled their obligation and came. Few, very few, seemed to be participating in Mass. They would come in and sit in "their" pew, chat with their friends and acquaintances around them, check to see who was and wasn't there, fill out their checks for the weekly envelopes, and read the weekly bulletin. They came to Mass as if this was an event outside of themselves. They would stand in line for Holy Communion and then dash out the doors. One Sunday, I felt called to say something about this matter.

"Good morning," I said. My words were met with a smattering of muffled "good mornings." No one was really listening as they had other things to do. I said it again, this time a bit more loudly, which startled quite a number. Now their response was quite different. Instead of beginning with the usual welcoming, I asked a question.

"When was the last time you received a love letter? Better yet, when was the last time you wrote one?" The silence in the sanctuary was deafening. Everyone had stopped what they were doing. They were listening. To change a set pattern will sometimes get people's attention. "What's in a love letter?" I continued. "The one writing it is telling the beloved the why, how, and the depth of their love. The author also tells the recipient about her or himself. The recipient feels, or should feel, the honesty, passion, and love of the author." I was now holding up my Bible. "Well, each Sunday we come here and have three love letters from the Author of Creation. He tells us and shows us how much He loves us and why. All He is asking is that we love Him in return. Perhaps one or more of these love letters today is for you. Listen to them and understand what they say and the depth to which Our Creator loves each one of us."

As I spoke, I was not concerned with the reaction from the parishioners in the pews nor from the priest about to say Mass. I didn't intend to be praised or condemned. I said what I believed I was called to say. After Mass, a man in his mid-fifties came up to me long after most had left. He told me that it was the first time in decades he had listened to the readings and wanted to thank me. He said it made a lot of sense and made an impact on him. I figured if only one person heard and understood, that was what God wanted.

Practical Business Ethics

Work was going well, in fact, too well. The number of investigative cases and their depth were increasing as well. An idea came to me, which I suggested to Larry, my boss. Rather than being reactive, I said, we should be proactive. I asked if I could develop a program that would make people think and be aware of the ramifications of breaking company policy. He was in favor of it, and I proceeded. I put together the program and called it "Practical Business Ethics." The goal of the program was to "prevent you from succumbing to the temptation to do something wrong."

I presented the program in Columbus, Ohio, for the first time while assisting in a large investigation in the area. I offered to present this to the organization affected by the investigation. The Vice-President of the organization thought it was a good idea. A conference room was set up and forty managers, all computer engineers, arrived. They begrudgingly took their seats. Some mumbled about another useless AT&T training program. There they sat, each in their short sleeves, their white shirts, ties, and pocket protectors. A tough audience indeed for my first foray. I introduced myself and began.

"I'm going to tell you why people do wrong things." A smattering of muffled curses came from a few. I blew it off. Then, leaning into them, I half-whispered, "And then I'm going to tell you how you get caught." The atmosphere changed immediately.

"How many of you have bought a lottery ticket?" I continued. Over thirty-five people raised their hands. "So, you would risk X to gain Y. Let me ask, who would bet one dollar to win one billion?" Every hand went up. "Keep your hands up. If you would bet ten dollars to win one hundred million, keep your hand up." Some hands dropped. I continued. "How about a thousand to win a million?" Only a few hands remained up. I asked all to put their hands down and asked, "Would you bet $250,000.00 to win twenty-five dollars?" No hands went up. "Any time you lie on an expense report or steal a box of pens, you are risking your salary, benefits, and reputation for a measly twenty-five dollars." The room was silent, and all were listening. I then asked them to stand.

"Take a look around at every other person in the room. Take a few minutes to look at everyone." After a few minutes, I asked them to sit. "Thinking of all those you looked at, is there anyone in the room who can say, in their heart, that they love every other person in the room?" One woman, a middle-aged black woman, raised her hand.

"Is the reason you said yes, a spiritual reason?"

"Yes."

"We should all be like you, but we're not," I continued. "There might be someone in this room that you do love, maybe even more than one. If you love that person, you, because you love them, will do everything in your power to prevent that person from doing something wrong, or if the person has done something wrong, you will, because of your love, try to get that person to rectify the wrong. That's what love is. It's sacrifice."

I went on, "If you like that person, depending upon the degree to which you like that person, you may or may not get involved. However, if you hate that person, and it doesn't matter why, you may hate them because they are too tall, too short, too thin, too fat, too black, too white—it doesn't make a difference—if you hate them, and you have found that they have done something wrong, do you know what you're going to do?" No one answered.

"I'll tell you. You're going to call me. How do I know this? I've worked over 2,300 cases, and I have never had to make a sales call. I have never had to go out and look for a case."

Their minds were racing. "Now, remember all those faces you looked at a few minutes ago? With your luck, who do you think would find out that you have done something wrong? If you had good luck, you would have already hit one of those lotteries. No, the person who would find out is the one who doesn't like you."

This was a presentation they hadn't expected. It was common sense and engineers appreciate that, as do most.

The primary reason I created this program was to prevent any employee from having to go home and tell their spouse and children they were fired. I'd seen this happen to many. Too many sad people realize their mistakes and what they face when they go home. They risk so much for so little. Regrettably, some lose more than a job; some lose their freedom. I wanted to prevent this from happening, and hopefully I did.

To drive my point across to them, I presented two cases of mine. The first was a case in which I received an anonymous call. The caller, a clerk, stated he had had it with managers in his business unit stealing from the company. They were lying on expense account reports. He provided me with a few particulars and names. When I called headquarters requesting the expense reports for these individuals, I wasn't prepared for what I got. I thought I would have received an overnight package, but instead there were five shipping boxes worth of reports. Daunting, to say the least.

As I unboxed the reports, I realized I wouldn't be able to remember all the expenses. Instead, I would have to remember to ask probing questions. Fortunately, we received computers a few months before. Several of the older investigators were wary of them and chose not to use them. I saw the future and decided to learn all I could about computers. One of the programs was an EXCEL-type spreadsheet program. It was a game-changer. Posting over six-thousand expense line items was arduous, but the spreadsheet provided all the tools I needed to ask the probing and proper questions.

One upper-level manager seemed to be the biggest culprit. He had been with the company for nearly thirty years. He traveled often and lavishly. One expense caught my eye almost immediately.

It was a five-dollar toll expense he incurred in, of all places, Milwaukee. It took four weeks to go through all the expenses in the Division. I had all the questions prepared for nearly twenty managers. I began by questioning the upper-level manager.

He was an A-type personality and proved it as soon as I met him. He thought he was going to oversee our conversation. "I have an eleven o'clock appointment, so make this quick."

"No problem. I have a few questions about these." I placed eighteen inches of expense reports on his desk.

"What the hell is this? Expense reports? I don't have time for this."

"Actually, you do. Your eleven o'clock has been canceled."

"What? Who do you think you are?"

I showed him my investigative credentials. "You are required, as a condition of employment, to cooperate in a security investigation." He had no choice. "Do you remember a trip you took to Milwaukee, Wisconsin, a few months ago?"

"Yeah, what about it?"

"You spent two days there, right? Did you check your luggage?"

Angrily he responded, "I never check luggage. I hate waiting for it. I want to get and go."

"OK. You rented a car. Hertz or Avis?"

"Avis, I always rent Avis."

I wanted him to remember as much as he could about the trip without looking at the reports. That he knew he had rented, Avis assured me he recalled a lot about the trip.

"Do you have to take one of those shuttle buses to get your car at the Milwaukee airport?"

"No, you walk right out of the terminal, and the cars are in the lot."

He was getting edgy. "OK, you got the car and drove downtown to the hotel. You paid the highway toll. Did you pay it when you got on the tollway or when you exited?"

"When I got off."

"Then you checked into the hotel, tipped the bellboy, and, well, let's go back to the airport for a minute. You said you paid the toll when you got off. Correct?"

"Yeah."

"Well, I lived in Milwaukee for seven years and can tell you there are no tolls in the entire State!"

He became flushed. He didn't respond immediately, but then composed himself. "Maybe it's a toll from another trip. I travel a lot for this company."

"I understand and would probably give you the benefit of the doubt, but that evening you had dinner at Chalet on the Lake, a very nice restaurant. I called there and asked for a manager. The man who answered said he was a manager. I introduced myself and he interrupted me."

He asked if I was the same Hugh McMahon who played for Marquette.

"In fact, I am." He went on for a few minutes about how he loved the team and the way I played.

Looking at the subject, I continued, "When he finished, I knew he would give me the information I asked for. I told him that I was conducting an audit and needed specifics on a meal that you had that evening. The restaurant manager asked me for the date and said he'd be right back. After a few minutes, he had the receipt. 'Dinner for two,' he said."

'No, dinner for six. I have the names.'

"The restaurant manager then went about reading the selections on the bill. Dinner for two for nearly $400.00."

"I've checked the names you put on your expense voucher. One of the names is an associate of yours back in Dallas. Well, while you claim he was with you in Milwaukee enjoying dinner, he in fact was in Portland, Oregon, having dinner with you! How is that possible?"

He slumped in his chair. He knew he was caught. I told him, based upon my investigation, he owed the company in excess of twenty-thousand dollars just for the vouchers I'd examined. He looked at me with imploring eyes. The type A personality was gone. He was looking for a lifeboat."

The engineers listening to this report were spellbound, and some, I think, were hoping I wouldn't investigate their expenses.

"He lost everything," I continued. "He lost a great job, a great salary, benefits, and tragically, for him, his pension. Nealy thirty years of working all went down the drain because he upset one person who had had enough and called me. Sixteen managers in the Division were terminated for similar voucher fraud during this investigation."

The second case I shared with them also came to me via a phone call. It was about drugs.

"A young woman from Human Resources called me. The Division she worked for was a newly purchased subsidiary of AT&T. She asked if we could meet away from the office, and she'd like to bring a manager with her who would like to talk about the drug problem he knows of at their facility. A meeting was set for the following afternoon. We met at a small restaurant near their offices in the mid-afternoon when the restaurant was quiet. Introductions were made, and he proceeded to tell me an astonishing account about the drug dealing and usage at the facility."

I didn't go into details but shared with them that twenty managers lost their jobs, including the manager who brought this to light. He knew he was going to lose his job as he was using as well and saw no other way to stop using than to get away from it all and to come clean.

"Again," I commented, "someone called me about something that violated company policy and their conscience. Now, the people involved in these cases were, for the most part, good people who had done bad things. They got caught up and succumbed to temptation. All of us are subject to temptations. The question is, do we fight them off?"

These engineers were very appreciative of this presentation. "It makes you think" was the response of some, but I bet it made all of them think.

The old me would never have thought about doing an investigation and presenting the results to a group. I even talked about justice and spiritual matters. Imagine me, that street kid from Brooklyn, talking about God and faith in front of strangers! The new me knew I had to do it. Later that year, there was a conference held at AT&T Headquarters in New Jersey. The Corporate Audit and Security divisions were in attendance. There were speeches and awards. I was chatting with one of my security buddies when someone said to me, "Hey, McMahon, they just called your name. Go up there."

I stood and went up to the stage. The presenter gave me an AT&T award for "The Highest Standards of Integrity." I was stunned. Me? How could this happen to me? Again, this was God moving in my life. It's truly astonishing to see how your life changes once you truly start to believe and move towards God. It's like a path that, although filled with challenges and troubles, still leads to a bright light at the end.

Confession

It was a scary place when I was in second grade. The Confessional. You were in there, alone and in the dark. The kneeler was as uncomfortable as you were. You could hear some mumbling going on from the other side of the Confessional box, but you couldn't exactly discern what was being said. If you went with a friend or a sibling, you half hoped their sins would be worse than yours, so the priest wouldn't get angry and assign you a penance reserved for a fallen angel.

As you knelt, you were trying to remember your sins. If they were "bad enough," beads of sweat would begin to appear on your brow, and you thought to yourself, "I can't tell him that!" Then, suddenly, you hear the sliding screen close on the other side, and the priest slides open the side where you are kneeling. Here it is, you and the priest, and there's no escape. You try to remember how to begin: "Bless me Father for I have sinned."

The priest replies, "Yes, please begin."

And then you relate all the horrible things you've done, except those you're too embarrassed to tell.

And the priest says, "Is that it?"

"Yes. Father," you respond. Now, here it comes, your penance! It might be a few prayers or a suggestion to ask the person you've hurt for forgiveness, and then the priest asks you to say an Act of Contrition.

As you say it, he's praying, and at the end he says, "I absolve you of your sins. Go in peace."

And that's it. You've done what you think you needed to do for your mom or your nun. You're good to go.

That, my friends, is the immature and unknowing reason to go to Confession. We learned this "ritual" when we were young and went through the motions and rubrics. As we aged, we went less often as the ritual didn't seem to have much of an impact. As we went less, we figured we didn't have to go and ask for forgiveness. We could either go directly to God or blow it off since what we did wasn't really a sin, and if it was, it was just a minor infraction. So we told ourselves. This drifting, and drifting away, leads us to rationalize everything we do. "It's no big deal." That's an expression we use for ourselves to brush off the things we've said or done. "Nobody got hurt," or "Everybody's doing it." These excuses become comfort zones for us. That comfort zone comes back to bite you when you least expect it.

When Christopher died in 1986, I returned to Dallas, vowing to go to Confession. He was a great young man who I loved, and I wanted to see him again. Knowing my past, I needed to go to Confession; really go. I had to confess all that I had done. Well, I did. I met with a young priest at the back of the church and told him all I could remember about my past life. It took a while. When I left, I was glad that I had gone to Confession, but. . .I did amend my life, but there was something missing. I did feel better about myself, but there was something not right.

A few years past and, as I grew in my faith and grew in the knowledge of Who God is, I knew I had to go to Confession again. In the Act of Contrition, a beautiful prayer to say when you're not rushing, there is a line that impacted me greatly. Here's the prayer and the phrase underlined:

> *O my God, I am heartily sorry for having offended Thee.*
> *And I detest all my sins, because I dread the loss of Heaven*
> *and pains of Hell, but most of all, because they offend Thee,*
> *My God, <u>Who art all good</u>, and deserving of all my love.*
> *I firmly resolve, with the help of Thy grace, to confess my*
> *sins, to do penance, and to amend my life, Amen.*

That phrase hit me like a ton of bricks. Yes, God *IS* all good; perfectly good, blessedly good, truthfully good, and here I was, for most of my life, offending Him who has loved me always and is all good. How devastating this was for me. This reality that I had offended the all-loving God Who is perfect. The weight of my sins came back to me as if I had been run over by a truck.

Going to Confession again, I realized why I was sorry and knew, in my heart and soul, that I was sorry, painfully sorry. I contacted a Jesuit priest here in Dallas. We met in his office. As I recounted all my sins, I sunk deeper and deeper into sorrow. I knew, however, I had to get them out, admit them. I remembered those I hurt, those I used. During the time I was there, 30 minutes or so, I began sobbing about the things I'd done and those I had hurt. The minutes ticked by, and as I shared my transgressions, the tears flowed uncontrollably. The realization of my actions, the hurt I had caused to both God and others, washed over me like a tidal wave of sorrow. It was as if every misstep, every hurtful word, and every selfish act was now laid bare before me, stark and undeniable.

As I recounted the last of my sins, my voice quivered with emotion. The reality of my wrongdoing hit me like a harsh truth that couldn't be escaped. I felt a deep ache within me, a regret that reached the core of my being. Despite my failings, God's love for me was clear, and I could sense the disappointment and pain I had caused. The faces of those I had hurt, the lives I had disrupted, haunted my thoughts.

By the time my confession came to an end, I was soaked in tears, a mix of shame, sorrow, and a burning desire to make amends.

Unbeknownst to me, as I was sobbing with my head in my hands, the priest had gotten up and had come over to me. I heard him say, "Are you finished?" I nodded my head up and down as I could no longer speak. He said to say an Act of Contrition. I said it slowly and most meaningfully. When I got to the part about God being all good, I was crushed again. I finished the prayer. With that, the priest placed his hands on my head and said, "For these sins, and for the sins of your whole life, you are forgiven!" I truly felt as though Jesus was there, placing His hands on my head and saying these words. I was forgiven—for everything I had done.

Stepping out into the world again, I felt like a burden had been lifted. The autumn day wrapped me in its cool embrace, and the wind seemed to carry away the weight of my past. The sky looked bluer as if a reflection of the forgiveness I'd received.

The air felt fresher, like a cleansing balm for my soul. Knowing that God had forgiven me brought tears to my eyes—tears of gratitude and redemption.

I realized that my repentance had opened the door to God's mercy. This understanding filled me with a warm sense of hope. It was a reminder that no matter how far we stray, a genuine heart can always find its way back to grace.

Since that Confession, as I have mentioned, I have had the opportunity to ask forgiveness for those in my past I've hurt or mistreated in any way. That wasn't part of my Penance, but I knew I had to do it. Every person I asked has forgiven me. It's a blessing beyond anything I could have imagined.

So, my recommendation is: Look at your life, look to God, Who created you and loves you. It is sometimes hard to believe that God loves you. I know. How could he love a mutt like me? I often asked myself that. Once I realized, knew, and felt that He loved me, specifically me, I was overwhelmed. Once you search, you will understand what it is you've done and what it is you need to do. I promise you. You will not regret it.

Winnie

A FEW YEARS LATER, another one of those God moments happened that remind you that he's always watching and protecting you. In 1995, my wife was sponsoring a lovely young lady who wanted to enter the Catholic Church. She was a Mormon but felt called to be a Catholic. The young woman's grandmother, Winnie, was a close friend of my wife's mom and asked if Bonnie would sponsor her granddaughter. The encouragement from her grandmother and the guidance of Bonnie brought this young lady into the church on Easter of that year.

After the ceremony, we decided to hold a small party to celebrate this wonderful occasion. Prior to the celebration, my wife's mom spoke to me about her friend, Winnie. I was quite surprised by what she had to say. Winnie hated God. Though she went, dutifully, each Sunday to Mass, she hated God!

I asked, "Why?"

My mother-in-law said, "It's because her husband, Otis, had died, and she was mad at God for taking him. She really loved him and is bitter about God taking Otis from her."

My only response was, "Wow!"

Winnie was an educated woman, a college graduate, and quite intelligent. She was also fierce. She did have a soft side but never exposed it because she thought it was a sign of weakness.

As chance would have it, I found Winnie sitting alone in the den on a sofa during the party. I asked if I could sit with her. Half reluctantly, she said, "Sure." After chatting for a few minutes,

I blurted, "I understand you hate God." She was stunned and sat open mouthed.

"Who told you that?"

"Well," I asked, "is it true?"

She turned to me as if preparing for battle and said, "Yes!"

"Why?"

"Because He took my Otis from me."

"What happened?"

She began telling me about how they met in college and how they fell in love. Though their lives weren't perfect, they knew that they loved each other and that they would grow old together. They had several children, but Otis was the center of her life. Then Otis got sick.

"What was it?"

"He got cancer. We fought it every day and I prayed every day, but he died and God took him from me!" She raised her voice in anger. I knew she wasn't angry at me, so I continued.

"Winnie, can I ask you something and promise me you won't get mad?"

She looked warily at me "I'll try. What is it?"

I took a breath, as I knew what I was about to ask might set her off, but I felt compelled to ask. "Winnie," I asked very slowly, "Winnie, how long ago did Otis pass away?"

"Ten years ago."

"Winnie," I continued, "Winnie, if you could have Otis back here, right now, sitting next to you, would you want him here?"

She looked at me painfully but not angrily, saying, "Of course I would!"

"Winnie, if Otis were here, he would be ten years sicker and in more pain. Would you want that?"

"Of course not! I want him back the way he was before he was sick!"

"Yes, I understand that and so does God. God loved Otis enough to bring him home."

She just looked at me.

"God knows how much you loved Otis and knows you still do. God loves Otis as well and he loves you. *HE* doesn't want you to suffer or to be in pain. God wants you to put the love you have for Otis into His hands. It's like that Allstate commercial 'You're in good hands with Allstate'. Place your love for Otis in God's hands, and then place yourself there as well. You can be together in that love you've always had and be there in God's hands. Two things I can assure you God will not do; He will not open His hands and drop you, and he will not clap His hands together and destroy you. He will gently bring the love you both had for each other to Himself. Your love will remain with Him and Otis until God calls you to Himself."

She sat there in tears. It wasn't my purpose to have her cry, but she was crying. No one had come into the den during our chat. Perhaps God had a plan to talk to Winnie and needed a vessel.

Two weeks later, my mother-in-law asked me what I had said to Winnie. All I said was that we had a chat.

"She is so changed! She's cheerful, happy, and full of life."

I just shrugged and smiled. Perhaps we all need to put ourselves into God's hands and trust Him. It makes this life easier to bear and easier to live. Why God chose me, I don't know, but He did.

Retirement and a New Chapter

I REMAINED AT AT&T until 2007; then I took an early retirement package offered by the company. I spent nearly 29 years with AT&T. It was a good opportunity then to begin another chapter and to wind down a bit. As it happened, in 2008, I took another corporate job with a logistics company in the Dallas area. It was in Security, and I thought I was a good fit. The young man I worked for, however, was the most unethical person I had ever known. Though he was the director of security for this company and was to be the standard bearer, he failed miserably. He had no problem having me terminate a woman who had inadvertently put a nineteen cents battery (yes, $0.19) in her work smock when going out for a smoke break, while he would go on junkets with vendors costing thousands of dollars. Hers was a mistake; his was a violation of policy. I lasted eight months and quit.

An Education

Sleeping in became a wonderful gift upon retirement; however, you can get tired of that very quickly. In 2010, I decided to do something I never thought I'd do. I enlisted as a public high school substitute teacher in Dallas. I could make a difference for some and make a dollar or two to save for vacations. Boy, what an education!

After two years of "learning the ropes," I figured I'd seen it all. How foolish of me! I received a frantic call one morning from one of the schools on my list asking if I could rush over, though the school day had already begun. The administrator sounded desperate, so I agreed to go.

Upon arrival, I received attendance sheets and many "thank you" comments from those in the office (which was very unusual). As I walked to the assigned room, I wondered what all the fuss was about. Entering the classroom, I was met with, "It wasn't us, Mister! The teacher went nuts!" Strewn all over the floor and the teacher's desk were papers, pens, pencils, and books. Though the kids looked a bit concerned, none of them thought to clean it up.

I barely had time to take attendance when the bell rang, and they bolted from their desks and hit the floor. The second period class was entering while I cleaned up. I could tell by the looks on their faces they knew what had happened. The teacher had had enough. She quit, in a rage, after 32 years. Fed up, she exploded and put in her papers, leaving this substitute with no lesson plan. Nothing.

What do you do with senior high school students who, for the most part, don't even want to be in school? I took attendance and looked at them. Half of them had already put earphones in, some put their heads on the desk to sleep, and a few, a very few, looked at me for direction. Then it hit me like a ton of bricks. I asked them a question.

"Do you guys want to have an adult conversation?" Those looking at me for direction appeared stunned that a teacher would ask such a question. A few others looked up, but none removed their headphones. Those that heard shrugged their shoulders and said, "Yeah, why not?"

"OK then, there's one rule, and ONLY one rule." They did what typical teenagers do when they hear, 'There are rules.' They don't want them.

"No, you'll like this rule; I guarantee it. You must treat each other like adults, treat me like an adult, and I'll treat you as adults. Fair enough?" Six or seven nodded okay, and one even said, "That's cool."

I asked a question that absolutely brought them to silence. I was quite surprised. "What do you want to talk about?" They looked at me as though I was from another planet. My guess was that no teacher had ever asked them that question. "We can talk about anything. Sex? Drugs? Marriage. Military? College? Work? Anything!" Well after seven minutes, they were all "talked out." I couldn't believe they hadn't any real interests.

As there were more than thirty minutes left in class, I asked them if I could ask them a question. A few more students unplugged and began listening. I had never done anything like this before, so it was new ground for me as it was for them. "What do you think will be the most important question you will ever ask of yourself and for yourself in your entire life?"

One young girl answered almost immediately, "Am I going to be happy?" Wow! You could have knocked me off my feet. I wasn't expecting that. I, rightly or wrongly, assumed she might not be happy, but I didn't delve. "Great question! I think we all want to be happy. "Do you agree?" I was looking around the room.

A few more dropped the earplugs, and others began listening. I sensed they knew this was different. It wasn't like normal school and they were interested. I continued. "Anyone else?" A young guy sitting in front of me asked, "Am I going to be rich?"

"Now we're cooking with gas! Anyone in here want to remain poor? Everyone I know wants to be rich!"

More and more of the students were listening and engaging. Finally, a large, smiling, young black football player, slouching in the back, asked, "Am I gonna play in the NFL?" Just looking at him, I could tell he was completely out of shape; he was just large.

"No."

Upset, he responded, "Hey man!"

"Listen, I know what it takes to be a ballplayer, a pro. You must sacrifice, sacrifice a lot. You have to say no to all the things you want to say yes to, and yes to all the things you want to say no to. You can't party, do drugs, drink, or smoke, and you must work harder than anyone around you just to have a chance. I can tell just by the way you're sitting that you don't care enough about yourself to make it. It doesn't mean you can't. It's just that you will have to change. No coach can do it for you, no teammate, parent, or girl-friend." I think he understood because he sat up a bit and seemed to be interested. He was the last to ask a question.

I then took the opportunity to say, "All of your questions are valid and worthy of consideration, but none of them is the most important question you will ever ask yourself in your entire life. Do you want to know what that question is?" I looked around the room and every single student, even those who had had their heads on their desks, were looking intently at me. Not one had earplugs in any longer. They all wanted to know!

"Here's the question." Placing my right hand outward and then my left, I said, "Is there a God or not?"

The room exploded.

"There ain't no God," shouted a few on my right. Others in the room were yelling just as loudly, "It's Jesus!" Still others, "It ain't Jesus, it's just God!" It took me 30–45 seconds to get them quiet and under control. I reminded them, "Hey, there's one rule," as I pointed with one finger. They all got the point.

"Since we have a wide array of responses, let's take them and explore them. Fair enough?" They agreed, and I proceeded.

"Let's take the position of those who say there is no God," I began. "If there is no God, then all we are, are random atoms hurtling throughout the universe, some of which slammed into this planet. Then, after millions or billions of years, these atoms merged and formed things. These things became birds, alligators, mosquitos, humans, fish, etc. If this is true, then ultimately, and I do mean ultimately, there are no consequences. You can do whatever you want to do, and ultimately, there aren't real consequences."

"For example, you could kill every person in this city; murder them. Eventually, you would be caught, tried, convicted, and sentenced to death. After a few appeals, you'd be strapped to a gurney, wheeled into a room, have a needle placed into your arm, and someone would drop a plunger and within minutes, you'd be dead. Someone would come and collect your body and you'd be thrown into a grave to decompose into fertilizer. End of story."

A young guy in the back of the room said, "Man, that sucks!"

"Yeah, kind of sort of! That's if there's no God—no consequences—this is it—nothing more." Most looked gloomy.

"Now, on the other hand, let's say there is this God, a Creator. Now, I'm not here to tell you it's the God of the Christians, the Jews, the Muslims, or any other faith. All I'm saying is let's look at the possibility that there is God, a Creator. Remember this, however: there can't be something in between—there can't be a half-God. There IS or there ISN'T. Okay?" Some nodded, but all were listening.

"Let's hold that thought for a minute." I looked at a few of the young men. "Did you ever work in concrete, or build a deck or a fence?" Some shook their heads yes. Looking at some girls, I asked, "Did you ever make a dress, a skirt, or make a whole meal for the family?" Most nodded that they had.

I continued, "That thing that you made or built, you put a lot of energy into it; your blood, sweat, and tears if you will. When you finished, you probably were justifiably proud. You might have thought, 'I did that!' Now, that thing that you built, made, or cooked, though you poured yourself into it, was not you. You were outside of the thing you created. It was not you! Wouldn't it make sense, then, that if this God exists and He created everything—the universe—that he would be OUTSIDE of the universe in order to have created it?"

I could see them all thinking and beginning to wonder.

"Okay, now hold that thought as well," I said. "Does anyone know how long it takes for a ray of sun to get to the earth?" None of them knew, as I expected, so I told them. "On average, it takes about eight minutes and fifteen seconds. Now, everyone I think knows what the Space Shuttle is, correct?" All seemed to know.

"The Space Shuttle travels at a speed of 17,500 miles per hour. If you were to travel on the Space Shuttle to the farthest star that scientists have found, way out in the universe, how long would it take?"

One of the girls responded, "About 100 years."

"Nah," I said, shaking my head. "It'll take a lot longer than that. Anyone else?"

A young guy in the front row said, "About a thousand years!"

"Nope, a lot longer."

Lastly, a young girl, seemingly frustrated with the guesses, said. "Okay, a million years!"

"Nope, do you want to know?" They did. "If you travel on the Space Shuttle, traveling at 17,500 mph, every hour without stopping, it will take 305 billion. . ." (I paused for effect) "CENTU-RIES!" They sat stunned.

"Okay, now, let's put this all together. If this God exists, and if he created everything—the universe—and if what is written in many books is true, The Bible, the Torah, the Koran, then there are consequences. Now, the consequences are this. You will be in one place or the other FOR EVER. We don't really comprehend forever, but we do have an idea now of a long time (305 billion centuries). These 305 billion centuries, compared to forever, are not like a grain of sand as compared to all the grains of sand on every beach, desert, and ocean of the world. They are as nothing, as compared to forever!"

With that, the bell rang to change classes. Nobody moved. Finally, a girl said, "I've been in this school for four years, and that's the first time I learned anything!"

I was glad she listened and told her, "Great. You were thinking, and that's the reason you come to school. You come to think!"

I had no idea that when I received the call that morning it would lead to a discussion such as this. I hadn't done anything like this before, nor had I planned it. I did realize later that God used me to talk to these kids. Everything just flowed without my thinking about it. A few kids in other classes asked me to talk about philosophical and spiritual matters, and at other schools at which I subbed, I did. Some teachers thanked me. They told me if they had talked about God, they would be fired. Years ago, I was sitting where they were, oblivious to the world. Would I have listened to someone talk as I did? Maybe, just maybe, I would have.

So, the question remains. "Is there a God or not?" Don't answer without investigating. Just saying there is or there isn't doesn't do you any good whatsoever. Once you have discerned and come up with your answer—the answer for you—that is the way you'll live your life, accordingly.

The four years I taught in public high school after my retirement were an education for me as well as for the students. I allowed the students to ask me any question at all so long as they were respectful, thoughtful, and sincere. Some were funny and some were out of this world. One day a student asked a question for which I wasn't at all prepared.

"Hey coach, do you think there is a Hell?"

He caught me off guard. He called me "coach" since I helped out with the basketball teams, and he was a member of the varsity. I knew he was sincere and wanted my opinion.

"Well," I began, "I do believe in Hell, but I don't know if it is the fire and brimstone described in the Bible, filled with burning lakes and the smell of Sulphur. It may very well be that, but for me," I continued, "I think Hell might be your greatest fear."

Almost every student in the classroom was looking at me in anticipation of something profound. They were all thinking and wondering for themselves if in fact there is a Hell. I presented them with a visual.

"Suppose that you died and appeared before God; just you, standing there alone before Him. God looks at you and then embraces you. You are overwhelmed by the sensation of pure love. That pure love is for you, and for you alone. You couldn't have imagined this while you were living on Earth. The embrace is warming, comforting, reassuring, and tender. You never want to be released from it. Suddenly, the embrace relaxes and falls from you. You no longer have that feeling of security and love. God then says to you, 'That is how I have always loved you. There hasn't been one moment in all of your existence that I haven't loved you and loved you completely. However, you didn't want that love. You wanted no love at all. You didn't want to share love or accept love. You wanted to love only yourself and disregard all those I placed in your life. You have always wanted one thing and only one thing; you have wanted you. Since this is what you have always wanted, this is what I am giving you. I am giving you—YOU.'"

I went on. "As God says this, you sense a darkness slowly enveloping you, as well as coldness. As it becomes darker and darker, it also now becomes quieter and colder. You are drifting further and further away as the darkness is now complete. The quiet has turned into utter silence. You can't hear anything, nor can you make any sounds. The coldness is even gone now; there's nothing, absolutely nothing. The sensation of time even ceases. You are suspended in nothingness. You then realize; this is your existence forever. You will have this nothingness forever. The thought of it devastates you. You realize that this is it. This is it FOR-EVER. You are dead, yet alive with the thought of what you could have had, and you will have that thought forever."

I paused and finished with, "For me, that would be Hell." They were all completely silent.

Another experience, or visual if you will, I shared with the students was this one.

"I visualized that I had died and was before God. Though God isn't a being as we are, He presented Himself in a manner resembling a human. He had a smile and approached me. He embraced me. It was overwhelming to feel that embrace of love. He then released that embrace and moved slightly back from me. 'Hugh, it's wonderful that you are here at home.'

He then looked over my right shoulder. The smile seemed to fade a little from His face. He then looked over my left shoulder. The smile now had all but disappeared. 'Hugh, where all those I put in your life to bring home with you?' Talk about having the rug pulled out from under you! Here I was standing before God and I had let Him down. I failed to acknowledge Him before others. I failed to tell others about Him. I was afraid of what others would say about me but didn't realize what God had planned for me to do while alive. I felt small, diminished."

I continued with the students, "What would Heaven be like without those you love? If they were not there? Would you do all you could to have those be in Heaven with you?"

As I shared this and asked the questions, they were silent, and I believe they were taking in all I had said. However, you never know if you have had an impact on someone. Did any of these kids really listen?

A few years after I finished teaching, I was in a store buying some dog food. A young man, about twenty years old, was working the checkout counter. I placed the bag on the counter, and as he was ringing it up, he said, "You're the 'cool' sub from W.T. White, aren't you?" White was the school where I subbed nearly every day for four years and the kids called me the "cool sub" because I would listen to them and talk with them.

"Yep, that's me."

"I remember that speech you gave about God. I really listened to you and it made sense. I started going to church and have a lot of new friends. They are good people and I want to be like them."

"That's wonderful. Keep going. Life is a gift." Leaving the store, I raised my eyes and offered a silent thank you to God. At that moment, a spark of hope ignited within me. If that young man had taken my words to heart, maybe others had too. It felt like a small ripple that could grow into waves of change, gradually shaping the world for the better.

Understanding that God can work through anyone, even through someone as ordinary as me, brought a profound sense of purpose. The notion that my actions could help guide others back to a place of belonging filled me with warmth. It was a reminder that each of us, in our own way, can contribute to a greater good and make a meaningful impact on those around us.

Choices

Throughout this book, you might notice a recurring theme. Choices. We all make choices. We all will come to a crossroads where we will make a life-changing decision. It might be marriage or a job or another significant matter. Everyone has them throughout life. Some of them are easy decisions, while others are brutally hard. During early life, we are confronted with simple choices (though they do not seem so at the time). Who to pick for my team? Which dress should I wear? Should I ask her to the dance?

As we age, the crossroads get a bit more difficult. Should I go to college? If so. Where? Can I afford it? Should I join the military? Which branch? Should I tell her I love her? Should I take the job offer or wait?

As mature adults, we look upon crossroads with not just ourselves in mind. How will this decision affect others? Should I marry him/her? Should we have children? All these crossroads make us who we are. Not deciding makes us who we are as well. Think about the decision(s) you didn't make. Someone else got the job, your seat in college, the girl. We make decisions throughout our lifetimes; some are unwise, some wise.

Years ago, I envisioned an event that may have occurred in the distant past. Christ was walking on a dusty road in Judea. He was walking and talking with His disciples. As he walked, others joined in and listened. The crowd grew to a substantial size. As he approached an intersection of two roads, He turned and looked at the crowd. They all fixed their eyes upon Him, perhaps awaiting a miracle.

Many were there to see Him do something, while others were hanging on every word. He stopped at the intersection and said, "I'm going this way." Many were disappointed they would not experience a miracle, and they turned back and went their way. Others, too, were disappointed because they were expecting profound words, and they turned left at the intersection. Still others who were there just out of curiosity to see what was going on turned right to "go into town" for some fun.

He turned and continued on the road He had chosen. He didn't chase after those deciding not to follow. He didn't scream at them and say, "You're making a mistake." He just kept walking in the direction He knew He had to go.

The biggest crossroad you will ever decide to take is this last one, not the choice of college, job, or spouse. The decision to follow Him on the road, despite all obstacles, despite all advice from friends or loved ones to turn back, despite all the insults, catcalls, and slurs others shoot at you. So, the decision is yours, much like those on the road years ago. Follow Him or not.

Portal

As I've aged, I've had a few health issues as most of us do. I've had eight surgeries. Cancers, back problems from sports, and exposure to the sun. These ailments placed me under the knife far too much. After one of my surgeries for cancer, I contracted West Nile virus! West Nile is a virus borne by mosquitos. The virus doesn't affect most, but if you are immune deficient as I was after the surgery, it can be fatal. I was admitted to the hospital and diagnosed with encephalitis (inflammation of the brain). I was becoming a medical book unto myself. Once you think it's all past, another thing comes at you.

It was 2018, and we had just moved to East Texas and settled into a golf community. Bonnie decided she wanted to learn how to play, and this would be perfect for both of us. Well, two months after arriving, I wound up in the hospital for a month. The first two weeks were spent in intermediate intensive care (IICU). My kidneys were failing. Fortunately, the doctors and nurses stopped the deterioration at Stage 3b, and I have been stable since. I did, however, have to go through chemo for the second time. My first bout with chemo six years before was for a malignant tumor in my left salivary gland. The surgery was to last two hours. It lasted seven. The tumor was removed along with thirty-five lymph nodes. My surgeon recommended chemotherapy and radiation since the pathology report indicated the tumor to be the rarest cancer in the world. The chemo and radiation had no lasting effects.

I thought this next bout with chemo for my kidneys would be a breeze as well. The chemo was brutal. It lasted seven months; five of which were outpatient. Something, however, happened while I was in the hospital for that month, in the quiet of an early morning.

Most of us, me included, go through our days without seeing the wonder of them. Simply breathing in and out, when you think about it, is a miracle. We never count our breaths, heartbeats, or blinks. They just "happen" in the daily course of life. If we took the time to measure them all during the day, we'd be exhausted and would not embrace those people and things that do come into our lives.

I was praying and thanking God for all that has come to me in life; the good and the bad, for it has all made me who I am. We choose the good and sometimes we choose the bad. It's free will, given to us by God as a gift. We don't think of freedom as a gift, but it is. While lying in the hospital bed, I thought about how I got here; not here in the hospital but how I got here—to Earth.

If God knew us before we were knit in our mother's womb, it would stand to reason that we existed in some fashion prior to conception. I thought of this and wondered just how we come into being. As I thought, I had a concept of coming to Earth through a portal, if you will. It's all I can understand, all I can explain. This portal is in some way like an infusion or injection. We are thrust into existence here on Earth. Bear with me here.

Picture this in your mind; our souls pre-exist, our physical condition and are awaiting our physical birth. Whether or not true, this is what I experienced while lying in bed. Our souls are joined to our bodies at conception, and we are born into human existence through this portal mentioned above. No matter where we are born, we are sent scattering into human/Earthly existence. The visual I got depicted millions of marbles, all cast upon a solid floor and scattered all about.

These marbles are moving at different speeds in different directions. Some marbles are flying at great neck speed, bouncing off other marbles and boundaries, not caring where they are going as long as they are exhilarated and flying about. They move far away from the Source and don't care about maintaining contact.

Other marbles are cautious and these are aware of the speeding marbles and their exciting far-flung lives. They see the wonders of that life but don't want to "go for that ride" as it poses dangers seen and unforeseen. They choose to be content playing both sides, enjoying some of the pleasures of the speed demons yet remaining anchored to their own comforts. They think little of the Source and bury any contact—at least for the moment.

There are also timid marbles, who, once thrust into existence, fear everything they see. They look upon the speed marbles as reckless, frightening individuals who only have themselves in mind and will crash and create havoc wherever they go. They look at the cautious marbles as those playing both sides against the middle; those wanting to be on the winning side when the game ends. These timid marbles are the judgmental marbles and think themselves always right and without fault. They believe they are close to the Source as they have never wandered far from their birth cave. They exist, but they don't live.

Finally, there are those who, for some reason, understand the Source and remain close always. These marbles are very few. However, these marbles exist all throughout human/earthly existence. They understand the other marbles and their ways, yet they don't judge. They understand that going back to the Source has only ONE passage: ONE gatekeeper. They remain focused on that gatekeeper while living this human/earthly life, and they try to point others to this ONE. The goal of our human/earthly existence is not the speeding or cautious or timid lives lived by so many, but our goal is returning to the Source. We can only return to the Source by going through the gatekeeper; the ONE. It's Jesus.

All, in their own way, are seeking happiness. Far too many seek temporal happiness and are not content with it once found. They are on to the next thing. Fortunately, some realize this before their lives end and turn to God. They find the Gatekeeper, and they find happiness, they find life.

We are provided with all we'll need to get home, back to Heaven, safely. As we live, we're tempted and succumb to these temptations—not all but a number of them.

I share this because I believe I've been guided to do so. For those who know me, I was one of the speed marbles for the early part of my life, bouncing about at breakneck speed and going nowhere fast. I had never thought of this before and some, most, or all of you might think I'm nuts, but it truly happened. I got this visual. I know now, who I am and to Whom I belong.

An Angel

THAT MONTH IN THE hospital gave me a lot of time to reflect on my life and life in general. Spending time in solitude is something we don't usually do. We're busy and anxious about everything. It's funny, but I wasn't anxious about anything while I was there. If this was "it," the end, then it was it. I've never feared death. It's inevitable, so why fear it? Going through a painful death would be hard, but dying itself shouldn't be feared. I had another unexplainable experience while in the hospital.

Not every spiritual experience takes place in a chapel, a Church, or other religious place. Sometimes such experiences happen most unexpectedly in most unexpected places. Lying in a hospital bed early one morning, 5:35 AM to be precise, I was awakened by the TV that turned on automatically. I was a bit startled as to why it went on and more startled that there was no picture!

I reached for the paddle to turn it off, but the effort was in vain. I tried every button, but the nurse call button. None could turn it off, on, or switch the channel. The channel was on EWTN, the Catholic channel. There were a few men talking about the pending canonization of Cardinal John Henry Newman. I began listening to some of the words written by Newman and realized they were for me, right then while lying in this bed.

The more I listened I realized God was speaking to me through Newman's words. I lay there listening until just before 6:00 AM when the TV automatically shut off! No more than 5 seconds later, a young child, 8 to 10 years old, was singing in the hallway outside of my room. The singing was beautiful and lasted 10 to 15 seconds. I didn't recognize the song—it was more of a lilt—a soft, joyful refrain. Then it was gone.

The nurse's aide came in right afterward. I asked her, "Who was that child singing?"

She looked at me and said, "What child?"

"The one right outside of my room. Is she still there?"

"There aren't any children on this floor; this is adult oncology, and visitors don't come up for hours."

Impossible, I thought. I KNOW I heard a child singing, and then it hit me. The TV, the message meant just for me, and this child singing—could they have been traces of an angel? The more I thought about what happened in those 30 minutes, the more convinced I was that it was an angel. I had been in the hospital for ten days by that time and had been doing a lot of praying—not for me but for my wife, sons, and many others. I believe God answered these prayers through the message I received via the TV and the voice I heard from the child. Prayer *is* communication with God. When listening, even at the most unexpected of times, He will answer. I need to do much more listening!

Imagine me, that street kid from Brooklyn, thinking about such things. Sometimes it's just overwhelming.

Among the many experiences I could recount, I'll conclude with this one. It was one of those moments of quiet reflection, where simply listening held a deep and powerful lesson.

The Tree

EVERYONE I KNOW HAS questioned themselves during their lives. Decisions are hard to make when emotions and lack of knowledge are part of the equation. What to do? Why am I stuck here in this job? I don't feel as though I should be here; it's not *me*. These thoughts grip you, leaving no immediate answers, maybe none at all.

For example, trying to guide teenagers through life feels like threading hope through a needle's eye, and, sometimes, like trying to untangle a mess in your mind. It's a mix of uncertainty and the struggle to convey complex truths in a way that makes sense.

At 18 years old, every kid feels immortal, and most think they'll never age. I asked myself: What would I have to have heard when I was 18 that would have had a definitive impact on my life? The idea of a tree came to me. Looking at a grand, old, stately oak tree gave me the idea of challenges in life, and perhaps, just perhaps, the metaphor gives clarity to this idea.

As we grow out of adolescence, we begin to make decisions for ourselves. These decisions, good and bad, begin to form us and set us on our path in life. The trunk of the tree is our launching pad if you will. It is our safe harbor, our strength, our source of nourishment. For Christians, this source is Jesus. As we climb up and out onto the limbs and branches, we learn many things. Some are lucky to have found that branch early in life and they are content with it. For example, a young girl knows almost immediately that she wants to be, or must be, a doctor. She gets on that path early and knows she is on the right branch.

Most of us, however, find ourselves on the wrong limb, yet we keep climbing out along it as it becomes a branch, and then a smaller branch and eventually a twig. When we've reached the end of the twigs, we realize that this is not where we're supposed to be. Now the question is, what do I do? Well, there are options, a few of which will satisfy us or make us content or happy.

First, we can remain there, at the end of the twig, and hope that something happens to improve our situation. We look at other limbs, branches, and twigs and think, 'If I was only over there.' Remaining in place and doing nothing is a choice, albeit it is a bad one.

Second, we stay there at the end of the twig and complain or suffer in silence. Neither of these is a good option. We could attempt to jump over to another twig, which looks attractive to us, with the hope of grabbing it and finally finding happiness and contentment. This can be very risky if the twig is too far away, or out of our grasp, and we could plummet down.

Third, we can slide down off the twig, and go up onto another twig on the same branch, in the hope that this is it and will be the right destination. Moving onto another twig on the same branch doesn't really change the view, though, does it? Going from twig to twig, or even branch to branch, usually doesn't get us to where we want to be or need to be. What is the solution? Is there one?

In many ways, the search for God is something like this. Christianity is like this. Some, the very fortunate ones, find faith in Christ early on in their lives. They live their lives accordingly and are seemingly at peace in all they do. Others struggle for a while and perhaps find their faith in their twenties and understand, as mature adults, the depth of faith and therefore live by it.

Some are rumbling through life, searching for successes and rewards, but they have this gnawing feeling that there is something else, something more, and they ask, 'What is it?' They too find their faith. It could be in their 50's or even 60's. They look back, for a moment, with regret, but they are at peace with what they have found. Lastly, some may find it when nearing death. They look back on their lives and question many things; one of which is possibly Eternity. At those moments, they can receive great faith and peace.

Wherever one might be in life, their branch might not suit them, and they may struggle to find that branch where they should be, where they should have been all along. Not all choose to search; some sit perched on a branch and are content with unhappiness. Perhaps they feel sorry for themselves while others rejoice at their choices and positions on the tree.

God has an abundance of graces and gifts for each of us if we only seek Him out. We can do this by finding the branch He created for us. I know where I am on this tree and am at peace. I'm not at the top or the bottom though it really doesn't matter. I am where I am supposed to be.

Finally, when you are in doubt or fear, always return to the trunk, that is, return to Jesus. He is rooted in God the Father and shares His love with us.

This has been my journey. When it will end; I really don't know. There will be more bumps in the road, no doubt, and blessings as well. My most recent bump is that I begin another round of radiation for another cancer. I'm not concerned about it as I don't fear death. I haven't feared death since that day in Coney Island in 1952 when my father screamed at me to pick up a gum wrapper and concluded then that my father didn't like me. Even then I thought, 'Why live, if you're not loved?' It took a long time to realize that I was loved and loved by God. Once I realized that, I still didn't fear death, but for another reason, as I knew everything would be alright.

Have there been regrets? Of course. In Sinatra's song, "My Way," this line has always had an impact on me: "Regrets, I've had a few, but too few to mention." Yes, there have been regrets. All rational people have them. I once dated a girl who told me there's nothing that she has ever done that she has regretted. Sad, I thought, and how cold. She has, as we all have, hurt people, yet she never regretted it. I hope she has changed. No one I know doesn't wish they could go back and change something or many things in their lives.

Some regrets I've recounted in this book. I regret I didn't have a father who knew how to love or to encourage. He hated his life and took it out on us. I regret I didn't see that lack of love earlier in life so that I could have been a better son. I regret I didn't know what true fatherhood was; perhaps my sons and I wouldn't have such a fractured relationship.

I am, however, very proud of my sons; all of them. They have worked through tough times and have found their niches in life. Mike, my eldest, has been in the U.S. Army for more than twenty years, serving our nation. Brendan has found that he is a great salesperson, working in international sales in Sao Paulo, Brazil. James spent eight years in the U.S. Air Force and then graduated from the University of Oklahoma. He works for CACI on technology for national security. Matthew was in the U.S. Navy for five years and then received a degree in cyber technology. He works as a cyber security analyst for a firm in Colorado. How could I not be proud of them?

I regret that I didn't realize that I could really learn things academically. I regret that I didn't tell the girl at AT&T how I truly felt. I do realize now, however, that telling her then, in the state that I was in, may have been a disaster because I was a disaster. I wanted it to be perfect, but it couldn't be.

The Table

THE BEST WAY I can explain perfection is with a metaphor. It's as if God was a fresh, new, white linen tablecloth about to be placed on a large dining room table. I was the table. I had a broken leg and three wobbly ones. The tabletop was filled with broken wine, whiskey, and beer bottles. There were ashtrays filled with burning cigarettes and cigars. There were sharp broken knives strewn around the table. Placing that white linen onto the table would have shredded it. The stains from the wine, whiskey, and beer would have ruined it. The knives would have cut through it. Yes, it would have been a disaster as the table was not fit for the cloth. The table had to be fixed. The table needed a Carpenter.

I found the Carpenter, a Master Carpenter. He swept away all the broken glass from the broken bottles, removing the ashtrays and burning cigarettes and cigars that had fallen onto the table. He removed the broken sharp knives. He came and fixed the broken leg. He repaired the wobbly legs. Once He did this, the table was on a solid foundation again. The tabletop was now ready to be cleaned. There were scratches made by the broken bottles, burns made by the cigarettes, and deep wounds made by the knives.

He painstakingly dug out the shards of glass and discarded them. He filled in the gouges left by the glass and knives and smoothed the surface. He prepared the tabletop for sanding. The sanding took time, and it was, at times, painful. He had to make certain all the marks were removed. He then stained it to its original color. Once he did all of this, He sealed the tabletop.

The table was almost ready to receive the white linen table-cloth. He placed upon the tabletop table pads. These pads would be a buffer to prevent any broken bottles, burnings, and gouges from getting to the tabletop. These pads were Himself, the Master carpenter. The tablecloth could now be spread and the table set. The clean, bright, pressed tablecloth is God, Our Father, covering me and all who ask this of Him.

Now, there will be times that the wine may spill, cranberry sauces drip from a plate, or even those darn lima beans will be squashed onto the cloth. I don't worry about it now, as I know the table pads will prevent the stains from becoming permanent. Some of the wine or cranberry sauce may leave a remnant of a stain on the pads. The tablecloth, though, remains clean. For these stains on the pads, they are like Purgatory, which can remove the remnants, to burn off the dross, so that we are perfectly present-able to God our Father.

Taking the Leap

I THANK GOD FOR many things: for four great sons; for Bonnie, a wonderfully loving wife; for a healthy body to play basketball, for I truly loved playing and meeting so many great guys; for wonderful jobs; for wonderful loving and forgiving friends; and for God finding me under that rock and giving me a chance to return to Him. He leaves the door open for every one of us to return. My advice is to slow down and take a look at who you are and what you were created for and created to do. Once you find this, you too will be at peace and be happy here and in the hereafter.

As I've said, I am at peace. No longer do I live in fear. I haven't since that day I heard God say, "Live the life you are supposed to lead." Just as in the photo below, as I leaped to grab a rebound of a teammate's missed shot, so I took that leap of faith in God. And just as I scored the basket on that rebound, I scored when I chose God above all things. I remember that moment when I leaped for that rebound. It was thrilling, and the crowd cheered wildly. That thrill was surpassed the next morning upon awakening to see the photo below in the local newspaper. I believe that awakening will be again surpassed when I leave this world and wake to hear God say, "Welcome home, good and faithful servant. You made the team. Go pick up a uniform!"

—Journal Photo by John C. Anderson

UP AND AT 'EM — Hugh McMahon of Marquette was all alone as he pursued this rebound against Xavier at the Arena Saturday night. The Warrior towered over Tom Blizegar of Xavier. Marquette won, 82-73.

Epilogue

CONTEMPLATIONS

I HOPE *MY JOURNEY* has made you think of your own life. You may have other questions to which you need answers. Here are a few questions you might consider helping you on your Journey:

Is there a God or not?

    a. There either is or there isn't anything in between couldn't be God.

Did this God create everything there is?

    a. He did or He didn't. If all of this just "happened," how did it start?

Is Jesus Christ God's Son?

    a. He either is or He isn't.

Did Jesus Christ die on a cross?

    a. He either did or He didn't. Roman, Jewish, and Christian history claim He did.

Was He buried?

    a. He either was or He wasn't.

Did He rise from the dead?

a. THIS is the critical question for all Christians and all of humanity to ponder.

b. He either did, or He didn't.

Did He ascend into Heaven?

a. He either did or He didn't.

Is He coming back?

a. I'll leave that for you to decide.

If all that was prophesized and written about God is true, including Eternal life, it might be well worth your time to consider and reflect upon the questions above. If none of it is true, then this existence is pretty much a waste of time. After all, who in their right mind would want to go through all the suffering, sickness, mental torment, and disappointments in this life if there is no hope of an afterlife and of meeting God?

And so, my journey continues, yet it is no longer one of fear. It is one of hope and faith.